Arguing it Out

The Natalie Zemon Davis Annual Lecture Series
at Central European University, Budapest

Series Editor: Gábor Klaniczay

ARGUING IT OUT:
DISCUSSION IN
TWELFTH-CENTURY
BYZANTIUM

Averil Cameron

Central European University Press

Budapest – *New York*

Published in 2016 by
Central European University Press
An imprint of the Central European University Limited Liability Company
Nádor utca 11, H-1051 Budapest, Hungary
Tel: +36-1-327-3138 or 327-3000 · *Fax:* +36-1-327-3183
E-mail: ceupress@press.ceu.edu · Website: www.ceupress.com

224 West 57th Street, New York NY 10019, USA
Tel: +1-732-763-8816
E-mail: meszarosa@press.ceu.edu

ISBN 978-963-386-111-0

Library of Congress Cataloging-in-Publication Data

Names: Cameron, Averil.
Title: Arguing it out : discussion in twelfth-century Byzantium / Averil
    Cameron.
Description: Budapest : Central European University Press, 2015. | Series:
    The Natalie Zemon Davis Annual Lecture series at Central European
    University, Budapest | Includes bibliographical references and index.
Identifiers: LCCN 2015030130 | ISBN 9789633861110 (alkaline paper)
Subjects: LCSH: Byzantine Empire—Social life and customs. | Byzantine
    Empire—Intellectual life. | Byzantine Empire—History—Sources. |
    Byzantine literature—Criticism, Textual. | Discussion—Social
    aspects—Byzantine Empire—History. | Dialogue—Social aspects—Byzantine
    Empire—History. | Discourse analysis—Byzantine Empire.
Classification: LCC DF531 .C27 2015 | DDC 949.5/02—dc23
LC record available at http://lccn.loc.gov/2015030130

Printed in Hungary

Table of Contents

Preface

I first encountered Natalie Davis in the late 1970s when I was lucky enough to spend a year at the Institute for Advanced Study in Princeton. Sabbaticals were not so common in those days, and that year was a turning point for me in several ways. Among them was the opportunity to attend the Shelby Cullom Davis seminar in the History Department of Princeton University, during the ascendancy of its founder, Lawrence Stone. Having been trained as a classicist and practising as an ancient historian, I was exposed in that seminar to an exciting world of interdisciplinary social history and anthropology, the latter represented by Clifford Geertz, whose seminars I also attended at the Institute. Natalie Zemon Davis had only recently arrived at Princeton from Berkeley, and had not long before published her collection entitled *Society and Culture in Early Modern France* in which she extended the realm of social history in exciting new ways. She included such themes such as ritual, symbol, carnival, religious rioting and the reversal of women's roles, all of them immensely fruitful. Much later, in the winter of 1994 to 1995, the academic year in which I had taken on the hitherto very male role of Warden of Keble College, Oxford, Natalie came to Oxford as George Eastman Visiting Professor and we renewed our acquaintance. She had by now published not only *The Return of Martin Guerre* but also *Fiction in the Archives. Women on the Margins* was published during that academic year.

A little later Natalie wrote in her Charles Homer Haskins Lecture of 1997 of the heady time in the early 1970s when women were struggling to become accepted and to find a place for the history of women on the academic agendas of American universities. Again this was something with which I could identify, and which I had encountered in its first stages in another North American context. That was during an earlier and very memorable year spent teaching graduate students at Columbia University in New York in 1967–68, a critical year for race, gender and the politics of protest. In those far-off times North American women classicists were themselves conducting a campaign for equal inclusion in the annual professional conference of the American Philological Association, held that year in Atlanta, Georgia. They came up with the idea of a women's caucus, an idea that was new to me at that time.

Natalie's and my paths did not cross again after our encounter in Princeton for almost another twenty years, when she was the George Eastman Visiting Professor in Oxford for 1994–95 and I had just become head of Keble. Natalie was the guest at a dinner for historians in my college, and she had written to me during the summer to tell me of her appointment. Meanwhile my work had focused increasingly on the eastern part of the late Roman empire during the period when when late antiquity was becoming established as a new and exciting historical challenge. Later still, I carried my enquiries into the Byzantine period, which is also the subject of the lectures I was invited to give in Natalie's honour at the Central European University in October, 2014.

Byzantium in the twelfth century may seem very far from the early modern period that Natalie has made her own. Yet her example and the avenues she opened up have never been far from my own consciousness. When choosing my topic I hoped that she might find in it some resonances with her own work, even in the different world of Byzantium. This was a period in Byzantium of great cultural vitality on which many new assessments are currently being produced, and when Byzantium's connections with the west and its broader Mediterranean context were both deepening. It was no longer—if it ever had been—a distant, exotic and non-European society. Thus it seems very suitable for the sort of cross-cultural approach that Natalie has opened up.

My argument here starts from a kind of literature that has not so far seemed important enough to be included in this new wave of publications on the literary and intellectual culture of the day. My question focuses on the prose dialogues in Greek from this period—of very varying kinds—and on what they can tell us about the society and culture of the long twelfth century, just the period, we need to remember, when western Europe was itself developing a new culture of schools, universities, and scholars.

We cannot forget, of course, that the Latins of the Fourth Crusade, these very westerners, turned on the Byzantines in 1204, sacked Constantinople and took its most precious treasures home with them. Seeing some of them again very recently in the treasury of San Marco in Venice brought the sheer level of plunder home to me with great force. A Latin patriarch and a Latin emperor replaced the Byzantine ones, and a Byzantine government in exile was set up across the Bosphorus at Nicaea in Asia Minor. However, Latin rule was not a success, and the Byzantines were able to return to Constantinople in 1261. Awareness of these events among modern scholars, as well as the huge attention given in modern research to the Crusades themselves (the First Crusade was launched in 1096), often affects, and can stand in the way of, the manner in which twelfth-century Byzantium is viewed. Yet this was also one of the most brilliant and culturally intense periods in the entire long history of Byzantium. I hope to show, or at least, given this brief compass, to suggest through the lens of contemporary literary dialogues, that there is more to it than has been so far revealed. The cross-cultural and imaginative paths that Natalie Davis has opened up for Europe in the early modern period, and the "culture field" and "terrains of polemic and encounter" of which Miri Rubin wrote in her own Natalie Zemon Davis lectures,[1] apply to Byzantium just as much as they do to the west.

One of the underlying questions in what follows is indeed the theme of European culture and society: does Byzantium belong to it or not? I contend that Byzantium deserves its place in the broader development of Europe, even as it also reaches out to the vast territories of Anatolia and the Caucasus, and to the eastern Mediterranean. The mixing, movement and encounters of individuals and peoples are major themes in Natalie Davis's recent work, and encounters between Greeks and Latins, Greeks and Armenians, and of Christians with Jews and Muslims are central to twelfth-century Byzantium too.

It was therefore an immense pleasure to receive the invitation of Gábor Klaniczay to deliver the Natalie Zemon Davis lectures at the Central European University in 2014. I had not then realized that Natalie herself would be present throughout the week during which the lectures were given, or that she would take such an active and energetic role in all the discussions and gatherings that took place, including the several formal and informal meetings that had been arranged with the diverse and highly intelligent graduate students at the CEU. This was an enormous pleasure and privilege and I value it tremendously. With her warmth, curiosity and energy Natalie is a real inspiration.

Besides thanking her, and thanking Gábor Klaniczay, himself a distinguished medieval historian with cross-cultural sensitivities, there are many others who made my stay so rewarding, and who have continued to help in many other ways. I have paid several visits to the CEU over the years, including participating in a summer university in 2004 and giving an invited lecture on dialogues, prefiguring the theme of this book, in May, 2012. Each time I have admired its ethos and ideals, and enjoyed meeting its excellent students. This visit was no exception.

I am particularly grateful to the wonderful Csilla Dobos, who not only arranged everything in practical ways but also looked after me with great kindness. Nóra Vörös of the Central European University Press has made the publication process unusually easy and straightforward. I also thank Niels Gaul and Volker Menze, both old friends, for their warmth and hospitality while I was in Budapest, as well as for many discussions on academic matters. It is a great pleasure to me that Niels Gaul and I have also collaborated in a workshop on dialogues held in Oxford earlier in 2014. During my stay in Budapest I was able to attend the meeting of the international Board of the Center for Mediterranean Studies, which brings together a wide range of departments and interests in exciting ways. I was also able to be present at a workshop co-organised by István Perczel, another old friend, with my former student Hagit Amirav, now a professor at VU University, Amsterdam. I was able to talk with György Geréby again both in Oxford earlier in the year and during this visit, and Aziz al-Azmeh was as kind a colleague and host as ever. The graduate students whom I met during my stay were as before a stimulating and interesting group, and I thank them for their warm friendship and the reception they gave me.

Other friends and colleagues have again been wonderful sources of help and information. Among them

I thank Niels Gaul again for finding time at a busy moment to read and provide valuable comments on my text, Nicholas de Lange for reading chapter three and providing many insights and comments based on his ongoing work on Byzantine Judaism, Alessandra Bucossi, the editor of the first critical edition of part one of a key work, the *Sacred Arsenal*, for sharing so much of her work as it developed, Guy Stroumsa for friendship and inspiration, Athanasios Markopoulos for sharing his work on education and teachers, Michele Trizio for his publications on twelfth-century philosophy and Alicia Simpson for pointing me in the right direction on Niketas Choniates. Many colleagues have shared their work with me, including Immacolata Aulisa, Nicholas de Lange, Katerina Ierodiakonou, Nadia Miladinova, Sébastien Morlet, Claudio Schiano and Paul Stephenson. Alberto Rigolio has again contributed valuable suggestions, and I must again thank Foteini Spingou for all the help she has provided in the course of my explorations into Byzantine dialogues and other Byzantine literary production, especially in a period for which I am perhaps not generally known. Obviously, as authors always rightly say, my mistakes are my own and there are no doubt many. I discovered while pursuing the theme of post-classical and Christian dialogues just what a huge field it is, and how much basic work still needs to be done. So what follows can only be a pointer. But I hope it will open up the subject to Byzantinists and others, and give them the urge and the energy to carry on the discovery.

Finally, I have spelled Byzantine names according to common usage, and so some are Latinized whereas others appear in Modern Greek spelling. This is a matter on which opinions vary greatly, but one on which I prefer clarity and convention to consistency.

Averil Cameron
September, 2015

Introduction

The chapters that follow focus on Byzantium and mainly on the elite circles of its capital, Constantinople in the long twelfth century: the Comnenian period, from the seizure of the throne by Alexius I Comnenus in 1081 to the sack of Constantinople by the Fourth Crusade in 1204. It is a period recognized as one of the most brilliant in Byzantine history in cultural terms, especially in terms of its literary production. Yet it was also one in which Byzantium felt the fateful impact of the Crusades, and which ended with the momentous sack of Constantinople by the Fourth Crusade in 1204. Despite revisionist attempts to play down the extent of this disaster, it was a blow from which arguably the Byzantines never fully recovered. Led by Michael VIII Palaeologus, they were able to return to Constantinople from their place of exile at Nicaea in 1261, and establish a renewed court and administration that lasted until the final conquest by the Ottomans in 1453. But the events of 1204 had brought fragmentation; lesser Byzantine courts were established in Epirus, in the Peloponnese and at Trebizond on the Black Sea coast, and the Palaeologan dynasty in Constantinople ruled over a state that was a fraction the size of what it had been, its imperial claims the more implausible given its miniature extent.

In contrast, and whatever challenges it faced, for most of the long twelfth century Byzantium was clearly still a major imperial state. Alexius I Comnenus had seized the throne in 1081 and founded the Comnenian dynasty, also establishing a new family-centred ruling aristocracy with a raft of new offices and titles. Alexius himself, his son John and his grandson Manuel were each lucky enough in the often unstable Byzantine context to have long reigns, and the three generations ruled in succession (admittedly not without difficult moments) for nearly a century. Even in the much more turbulent final years leading up to 1204 it was their descendants who still jostled for the throne. A flavour of the changing times, however, can be found in the vicissitudes of one of these, Andronicus Comnenus, before he seized the throne himself in 1182. In the previous decades he had been variously a captive of the Seljuk Turks, a fugitive at the court of the prince of Antioch and successively at those of King Amalric of Jerusalem and Nur-ad-Din, sultan of Damascus.

He married in turn Theodora Comnena, the widow of Baldwin III, and Agnes of France, who was still a child at the time. Having lived as a kind of royal adventurer, his short reign was brutal and his end grisly; a pogrom of Latins in Constantinople quickly followed after he became emperor, and his later excesses led to an invasion from Norman Sicily. Unedifying though it was, the life of Andronicus Comnenus exemplified the pressures from the west and in the east that weighed heavy on Byzantium in the period.

At the same time the age of the Comneni—the long twelfth century—was one of intense literary and intellectual activity. The output of members of the highly educated elite included poetry, letters, speeches, histories and chronicles, essays and theological treatises. The same period saw the revival of the Greek "novel," the Greek romance typical of the early empire and late antiquity. Love—the parting, vicissitudes and reunion of pairs of lovers—was the ostensible theme in these works, with a window-dressing of classical gods and heroes, and apparently innocent but actually suggestive descriptions, as well as some philosophical overtones. We have four such romances composed in prose and verse, drawing on earlier models and on the writers of the Second Sophistic of the early Roman empire. The culture of twelfth-century Byzantium could be described as hybrid in more ways than one. Were these new examples of romantic fiction in Greek influenced, as has been suggested, by similar compositions in the Latin west?[1] Was the culture of twelfth-century Constantinople therefore in some way derivative? That is Paul Magdalino's question (see chapter one below), and it is still a question worth asking. It is important for our subject that this was also the period when new schools, teachers and scholars were appearing in the west, with the development of scholasticism, and this impacted directly on Byzantium, when, for example, Latin delegations came to Constantinople to debate on theological matters and when their members displayed their new style of argument. I will discuss these debates in the next chapter. For now, it is important to realise that the intense literary culture of elite circles in Constantinople was a learned culture, steeped in classical literature and classical scholarship, and we shall need to understand its sources and its educational background in relation to these western developments.

The writing of poetry had already become a central activity for the educated elite in the eleventh century, and this trend continued during the twelfth.[2] Historiography and chronicle also flourished in the hands of John Skylitzes early in the reign of Alexius, the chronicler Cedrenus, John Zonaras, Alexius's daughter Anna and her husband Nicephorus Bryennius, John Cinnamus and the verse chronicler Constantine Manasses (also the author of a verse romance). At the end of the period Niketas Choniates wrote as an eye-witness about the sack of Constantinople in 1204.[3] These works could differ greatly from each other: Anthony Kaldellis describes Zonaras's chronicle as a "huge and severe 18-book narrative" but that of Manasses as "condensed, exciting and in verse."[4] Michael Glycas used the vernacular in his poems, but a more formal style in his chronicle. Anna Comnena, daughter of Alexius I, who composed the *Alexiad*, a eulogistic account of Alexius's achievements at home and on his military expeditions, was unique in Byzantium as a female historian, and indeed it has been argued that she has been given the credit for simply finishing the work of her husband, Nicephorus Bryennius. Bryennius also had historiographical pretensions, and has left a work known as *Materials for History* dealing with the period before Alexius came to the throne, commissioned by the empress. But as the daughter of the emperor Anna had received an excellent education, for which she thanked her parents in her will, and she was also fired by a filial desire to defend her father's reputation. Though her attempt, together with her influential mother, to promote her husband as Alexius's successor over the claims of her brother John came to nothing, not least it seems through his own lack of cooperation, and for the rest of her life, including the period when she wrote her history, Anna was outside the imperial inner circle. This did not prevent her from being associated with a group of learned intellectuals interested in Aristotelian philosophy[5] or from being regarded as exceptional. Even if some of her more outrageous claims are not to be believed, it would be a pity to deny her the credit for having written one of the most colourful historical works surviving from Byzantium.[6] Indeed, even if Anna was unusual, this was an age of powerful and influential women in imperial circles; some of them are also represented as literary and intellectual patrons, and must like Anna have been learned themselves.[7]

Letter-writing, of a highly literary and rhetorical kind, was also much practiced among the elite, and large numbers of letters survive from the period, even if no examples by women have been preserved. The rhetorical letter was one of the literary forms the Byzantines inherited from late antiquity, and a great deal of art went into its composition. But traditional or not, that does not mean that its content should be ignored, and in fact such formal letters are one of the best ways in which we can gain an idea of the social networks between members of the Constantinopolitan *literati*.[8]

They reveal a world of intense competition as well as personal connections. It was natural that the new

Comnenian court with its novel titles and promotion of clan relationships should act as a stimulus and motivator for those who wished to gain favour and advancement themselves—not the new "aristocracy" itself but the next level down, those who were dependent on the latter's favour. It is striking that the pathway was through literary production, assisted by the emergence of new schools, or rather teachers (for most "schools" in the period amounted to no more than the collection of pupils a teacher might gather around him). Though it is impossible to produce statistics, such was the hothouse environment that their rivalries and mutual competition, and their success or failure, determined the cultural and social atmosphere of the day.

This was not in itself new; recent studies by Floris Bernard and Stratis Papaioannou have pointed to a development that can already be seen in the eleventh century,[9] but the trend intensified in the twelfth century, and emperors themselves were participators as well as patrons. Alexius I Comnenus composed a somewhat cryptic work of his own, two sets of advice in verse known as the *Muses*,[10] and both Alexius and his grandson Manuel I took active personal roles in religious disputes, which included composing new treatises as well as taking part in the actual discussions.[11] Literary production at a high level required training material, in the form of rhetorical exercises, and there were public displays of rhetorical skill including contests between the schools themselves, with the aim of determining who was best in specific rhetorical tests.[12]

The voices of the lower classes are not often heard in this heady atmosphere, except when mediated through a commentator of higher social level. We find one of the writers of the period himself exploiting the persona of poverty by writing poems in the vernacular begging his highly-placed patrons for charity, but these are the productions of an intellectual and reflect the downside of the competition I have described. Sadly Byzantium does not offer us either the diaries or the archival material that Natalie Zemon Davis has used so brilliantly for later periods. For the lives of ordinary people we can look to the indirect evidence from saints' lives or apocryphal tales, or perhaps from homilies, or to some of the anecdotal material contained in collections of legal judgements surviving from the eleventh and thirteenth centuries. But Byzantine letter-collections contain the letters of the educated elite, not the kind of informal and personal material that exists so abundantly in the papyri of late antique Egypt, or for that matter in the rich Jewish documents found in the Cairo Genizah (although some of these indeed shed light on the Byzantine Jewish communities considered in chapter three).

So my subject here deals with the elite, and with the educated, and mostly perforce male, culture of twelfth-century Constantinople. It is a good moment for such a focus. This seems to be a critical phase in the study of Byzantine literature, with established scholars in the field planning major studies, and a new wave of younger scholars opening up exciting and original perspectives. In a recent paper Elizabeth Jeffreys states that the study of Byzantine literature is still under-theorized. She has also maintained that literature in Byzantium was essentially, or even always, utilitarian in character, that is, written to get a job, for a specific occasion, for preferment, or for competitive advantage.[13] Other scholars are nevertheless trying to find ways of applying literary analysis to the same texts, or asking themselves what kind of history of Byzantine literature could now be written. Clearly some key theoretical problems lie behind the attention now being given to literary production in the Comnenian period.[14] I find it striking that with the occasional exception of hagiography, works that fall into the category of theology or that deal with religious issues are usually left out of the discussion, even when they were composed by the same authors who also composed secular works, and these chapters will attempt to bring the different types of writing together.

9

Byzantine dialogues

I want to see in what follows what picture of that culture we can obtain if we consider a particular type of writing that has generally been overlooked, namely the literary dialogues. This is a type of composition that was produced during almost the entire Byzantine period, and yet which has made little impact so far in the scholarship on Byzantine literature and literary culture.[15] Yet the twelfth century produced its share of dialogues, and in considerable variety, and they need to be brought into the conversations about Comnenian literature and cultural activity.

Exceptions to this generalization are the literary dialogues on secular subjects, some of them usually described as satirical, in the general manner of the second-century Greek satirist Lucian, rather than distant descendants of the dialogues of Plato. These too have often been seen in terms of a literary revival, like the contemporary revival of interest in Plutarch. Even now however, they are not all easily accessible, and tend to be the subject of generalizations rather than detailed analysis.[16] I will draw attention in chapter one to some of these literary dialogues, examples of which continued to be produced in the Palaeologan period and even later. But they do not stand alone. Twelfth-century writers also cast theological and philosophical argument in dialogue form, even when they were dealing with current controversies where one might have expected that the urgency of the moment demanded direct communication. And dialogues—sometimes very lengthy—continued to be produced on the themes of Christian arguments against Jews and Muslims. Religious differences with the Armenians provided another topic, and the debates between representatives of the Latin church with Byzantine spokesmen that took place in this period produced a further, and increasingly important, range of subject matter. Formal debates took place in Constantinople or elsewhere in the Byzantine empire and were recorded at the time, or supplied the material for written compositions in dialogue form, which might or might not convey something close to what was actually said. Again, while some of these have been studied, though certainly not all, they have not often been studied by the same scholars who are currently active in addressing the literature of the period; sometimes too they have been of more interest to western medievalists, with their own scholarly agendas, than to Byzantinists. Of course there is also a long tradition of scholarship among church historians and theologians on some of their main themes, such as the question of the *Filioque* (the western addition to the Creed rejected in the Greek east), but this does not usually extend to the literary or social analysis of the texts in question. One of my main contentions in the chapters that follow will be that theological and religious writing cannot be taken in isolation from the lively secular production of the period if we want to understand the society and culture of Comnenian Byzantium as it actually was.

The aim of chapter one is to reinsert Byzantine dialogues into the literary production and the intellectual and social milieu of Byzantium in the critical period of the long twelfth century. I include a consideration of the methodology of social history as applied to Byzantium and ask how this can be modified by consideration of literary factors and discourse analysis; from this the chapter moves to consider the various different kinds of literary dialogue produced in the Byzantine context of the long twelfth century. Chapter two focuses mainly on the contemporary debates between the Orthodox Byzantines ("Greeks") and the representatives of the western church ("Latins") and the dialogue texts that were composed as a result, which frequently claim to present the debates as they actually happened. Chapter three turns to the continued composition in this period of dialogues between Christians and Jews and Christians and Muslims, and asks what lay behind them, how they relate to the actual dealings of Byzantium with Jews and Muslims in this period and how they interact with the Byzantine articulations of orthodoxy and heresy that are also a prominent feature. In the Conclusions I will try to bring all these texts together and to suggest that taken together in this way they not only reveal a world of tensions and argument, but that they too have agency in the cognitive experiences of contemporary Byzantines.

Dialogue texts and the world of Byzantium

Behind these enquiries lies an urgent and deeper question: what kind of analysis is appropriate in order to get a better understanding of this world, strange as it may seem at first sight to those not already familiar with it? More specifically, how might the literary analysis of these and other Byzantine texts help us to understand the nature of Byzantine society?

I think it is worth spending more time on the question, particularly in view of the fundamental historical developments that were also taking place in the period. Trying to place Byzantium, for example, in the broader and more transnational or global frame to which many historians now aspire demands a comparison with the intellectual and educational changes taking place in the contemporary west, just as consideration of Byzantine writing about Jews and Muslims

13

asks us to look beyond Byzantium itself and to the Mediterranean world, both east and west. As I point out in chapter one, some of the scholars who are dealing with literary production in Comnenian Byzantium are indeed approaching their material in social as well as literary terms, and considering such underlying factors as the educational system, the social networks, the workings of patronage and advancement as well as literary themes such as narrativity or the use of classical models and linguistic registers. All this new publication is immensely welcome. But given the many prejudices that still surround everything to do with Byzantium,[17] as well as its unfamiliarity to non-specialists, I believe that we need a more integrated approach. Chapter one begins therefore by asking how—or whether—these approaches can fit together, and what can be gained from drawing on the example of literary dialogues. What kind of dialogue literature was composed in twelfth-century Byzantium, and what might it tell us about the arguments and tensions within Byzantine society itself?

Chapter 1

Inside Byzantium

Early in the reign of Alexius I Comnenus a storm blew up in the higher echelons of Constantinople, when the emperor resorted to melting down church treasures to meet the pressing financial needs of his campaign against the Normans. He was opposed by a leading churchman, who stirred up feeling by writing round to members of the court, the imperial family and the church, claiming that not only religious images but also the material objects that carried them were sacred and could not be touched. Eventually and not without difficulty the emperor's wishes prevailed and the offending bishop was deposed. Amid the intense argument that surrounded the affair, with members of the clergy and the elite alike taking passionate positions, Eustratius of Nicaea, one of those who helped to support the emperor's case, did so in the form of a Platonic dialogue. He used it to reiterate the theory of images that had been accepted since the end of iconoclasm in the ninth century whereby only the image itself was sacred, not the material from which it was made,[1] The speakers are two characters named Lover of Truth and Lover of Habit. They meet in the street, fall into conversation, and then go to the house of Lover of Truth to continue their discussion about the controversy, which had led to the fall of a very eminent man. Continuing the rhetorical trope of *ethopoiia*, characterization, Lover of Truth—who needless to say prevails—is a veritable hermit, devoted to the search for knowledge, while Lover of Habit is always out and about in society. Being on the emperor's side, Truth wins the argument.

The emperor's opponent was a well-connected bishop, Leo of Chalcedon, who did not hesitate to call in his connections in high society when pressing his case. Although the emperor was eventually able to bring about his exile, Leo had managed to stir up a storm among the intelligentsia and the new Comnenian elite which no doubt had as much to do with rivalries and opposition to the new emperor as it did with the theology of images. Eustratius, the author of the dialogue mentioned above, and later the bishop of Nicaea, is an interesting figure whom we will meet again later. A philosopher and commentator on Aristotle's *Nicomachean Ethics*, he was praised for his learning by Anna Comnena (who may have commissioned his commentary). Anna describes how he debated with "Manichaeans," that is, Paulician dualists, while accompanying the emperor on campaign at Philippopolis in Bulgaria in 1114: "From early morning till afternoon or evening, sometimes till the second or third watch of the night, he [the Emperor Alexius] invited them to visit him and he instructed them in the orthodox faith, refuting their corrupt heresy. He had with him Eustratios, the bishop of Nicaea, a man with a detailed knowledge of religious and secular texts, more competent when it came to dialectics than the philosophers of the Stoa or the Academy, and also the archbishop of Philippopolis." (*Alexiad* XIV.8, transl. Sewter, rev. Frankopan)

She goes on, in an interesting comment that for all its partiality reveals that laymen as well as ecclesiastics took part in these debates: "The emperor's chief assistant, at all these interviews, however, was my husband, the *Kaisar* Nikephoros, whom he had trained in the study of the sacred literature." Eustratius escaped the fall-out from the condemnation of his teacher John Italus in 1082 but was brought down himself in 1117, not long after the debates at Philippopolis, when he was accused by his enemies of claiming that Christ argued in Aristotelian syllogisms. This time the emperor was unable to protect him, though he tried hard to do so by working with the then patriarch to lobby members of the Synod.

The latter episode is an interesting example of how even an emperor could fail to get his own way in this highly competitive environment. The disagreements that coloured relations between members of the elite during the period, including the court and the emperors themselves, were intellectual as well as theological; they can tell us something about how Byzantine society worked at these levels. It was a world in which theological, intellectual and literary issues intersected in the higher echelons of Constantinople with political, social and personal rivalries.[2]

In his attack on Alexius, Leo of Chalcedon had used the medium of letters to try to win people over to his side, and continued to do so even after he was exiled. Why then did Eustratius resort to the dialogue form? And who might have read what he wrote? While many scholars have already written on Byzantium in the twelfth century,[3] and the new trends in Byzantine literature and culture in that century are currently receiving a great deal of attention, no one so far as I know has addressed the literary phenomenon (also important for philosophy and theology) with which I am concerned here except in relation to some particular examples. The question, simply put, is why contemporaries thought it worthwhile to cast some of their literary output in the form of dialogues. What might this tell us about the intense cultural and intellectual life of Constantinople in the age of the Comneni and what means should we use to try to understand it? I will return to issues of religion in chapter two; but dialogues took many forms, and were not confined to high literature or theology. I want to start in this chapter by setting out the relevance of dialogues to any understanding of the intellectual and literary culture of the long twelfth century, and by raising the question about how we might now approach that culture.

The intellectual context

Understanding how Byzantine education worked at the higher levels of society is fundamental to our enquiry, and has been the subject of numerous studies, most recently a helpful survey by Athanasios Markopoulos, with up-to-date bibliographical references.[4] Its focus was on secular and classical literature and rhetoric, but some students will have studied a limited number of Platonic dialogues.[5] As in late antiquity and despite some imperial initiatives, "schools" centred on individual teachers and their pupils, and strong rivalries often developed between

19

them. The career ladder, to use an inappropriate modern term, was very slippery, and patronage was at least as important as education. Needless to say, the students were all male, except in a few special cases, and this education was not free; the teachers depended on payments they received. They also often taught in informal locations rather than in the special premises we expect today.

As we saw, many Byzantines in addition to Eustratius of Nicaea chose to express themselves in the dialogue form. Although I focus in these chapters on the long twelfth century, dialogues were composed in Greek throughout the history of Byzantium from late antiquity to the time of George Scholarios, Orthodox patriarch after the fall of Constantinople in 1453, who wrote dialogues himself.[6] Byzantines wrote more or less (often less) Platonic dialogues on both secular and theological subjects, and some drew on the satirical dialogues composed by Lucian in the second century AD for an immensely wide range of subjects, social, political and philosophical, with considerably more variation between their tone and character than the umbrella term "satirical dialogues" suggests.[7]

Several developments in twelfth-century literary culture can help us to understand some of these compositions, including a contemporary renewal of interest in Lucian, Plutarch, and other writers of the early empire and in the Second Sophistic. At the same time, along with the development of an intensely active literary culture went a variety of particular controversies and circumstances that made the effective presentation of an argument desirable, and perhaps particularly so if it was presented in a recognizably literary form. Some dialogue writers themselves commented on the appropriateness of the form for dealing with complex arguments. Finally, all this also took place against an increasingly demanding transnational situation, as I shall argue. The world around Byzantium was changing and its society was under many new pressures.

Given these features of the period of which these dialogues are a part, it is not surprising that twelfth-century writing is attracting attention from literary scholars, or that they are using new analyses to question the old stereotypes about Byzantium. Why writers composed what they did, how their works were performed (some at least were read out aloud in literary gatherings), who read them and who owned copies, are all questions vigorously pursued in current publications. The issues of who wrote these works and why are among the most fundamental of all. Surely the answers can tell us something important about how Comnenian society and culture actually functioned.

Social history and literature

Such a key period certainly demands a social analysis. Understanding elites is essential to understanding the Byzantine state, and the importance of great families in the Middle Byzantine period is already well recognized. It was this trend that had allowed Alexius I Comnenus to seize the throne, and his rule imposed a family-based model on government that worked well enough for a time, even if it was to prove dangerous later.[8] The "aristocracy" of the period has also been the subject of a good deal of scholarship.[9] But there is still work to be done before the literary and intellectual elite of the twelfth century and its composition can be incorporated into current scholarship on social history or the structure of the Byzantine state. For instance, the basic question "what is literature?" remains open. Paul Magdalino's lengthy and wide-ranging chapter entitled "The guardians of Orthodoxy" in his important book on the reign of Manuel I has the subheadings "birth," "books," "schools," "rhetoric and philosophy" (with the two treated separately), "judicial rhetoric and law," "medicine," "theology" and "a twelfth-century renaissance?," but not "literature."[10]

Whether there was a conception of "literature" in Byzantium, given all its overtones in modern usage, in certainly questionable, but it is a question not limited to Byzantium, but one that arises in relation to medieval writing in general. In contrast with Alexander Kazhdan's straightforwardly social approach to twelfth-century literature,[11] the definition of literature in Byzantium has been discussed many times recently, for instance by Panagiotis Agapitos in the *Oxford Handbook of Byzantine Studies*.[12] Some scholars would avoid the term altogether, but this tactic seems artificial as well as draconian. Thus Marc Lauxtermann has written of a "fundamental hermeneutic problem" and Stratis Papaioannou of a stage when there was a "potential transformation of rhetoric into literature."[13] Margaret Alexiou discussed the question from a narrow range of "literary" texts, while Ingela Nilsson writes both of "literature" and of "littérarité," referring to the "literary" features in Byzantine writing.[14] It is worth emphasizing in this context that a text written with a purpose can also be literary. Several scholars have also written of the twelfth century as the age when "professional" writers emerged in Byzantium, that is, individuals who one way or another lived by their pens.[15] The discussion is evidently still open, and one can only sympathize with Anthony Kaldellis when he says that what it means to read historical texts as literature is still unclear.[16] But even if scholars remain unsure of the answers, we can at least be sure that the questions "what is literature?"

23

and "what is authorship?" have finally arrived in Byzantine studies.[17]

How then should we approach the literary productions of twelfth-century Byzantium?

In addressing a topic that belongs so obviously in the elite world of the capital, and a way of writing that was practiced by a small and privileged group, I find myself outside the trend towards decentered history, about which Natalie Davis has written so well.[18] These chapters are not about local stories, or subaltern groups, and only partly about the wider cultural and geographical world outside Constantinople (although I argue that the texts do need to be read against this broader understanding). But the lively current scholarship on twelfth-century literary production, combined with the general neglect of dialogue texts, suggests that my topic is worth pursuing. Some students of twelfth-century Byzantine literature, like Niels Gaul in his study of Palaeologan writers and intellectuals, advocate a socio-literary approach, and similar efforts have been made to place their Comnenian equivalents in a social context. The works already mentioned by Floris Bernard and Stratis Papaioannou, for instance, emphasise the competitive nature of literary activity in period, which according to Macrides and Magdalino was led by "nouveaux riches" seeking advancement.[19] Kaldellis describes the historians of the period as mostly "imperial offi-cials, court orators and hangers-on," their works per-sonal rather than official.[20] Some had a patron, but this was not always the case, and it could also be dif-ficult to find one. How and why these works were written are key questions even if the wider social con-text is seldom raised.

It seems worthwhile then to spend a little more time considering the question of social history as ap-plied to Byzantium, and what kind of place in it, if any, is occupied by literary production. But we also have to ask which texts are candidates for this kind of analysis. A socio-literary approach is advocated for late antique literary production in a recent volume which has much to offer to Byzantinists, edited by Lieve Van Hoof and Peter Van Nuffelen.[21] Other scholars of late antiquity have already gone in the same direction, fol-lowing Elizabeth A. Clark's *History, Theory, Text*,[22] in which she describes her own move from an earlier ap-proach based on a social history that aimed at recover-ing "what really happened" to one based on the analy-sis of texts and discourse. Despite this, Van Hoof and van Nuffelen remark that most work on literary texts from late antiquity still focuses on strictly literary or even philological issues, what a text means and what tropes it uses. They also go on to say that the study of late antiquity still defines itself "in opposition to older visions of a general, political and cultural decline," that is, it has not yet claimed its own autonomy. If this is in fact the case for late antiquity, it applies even more to Byzantium. They also observe that scholarship on literature in late antiquity tends to concentrate on a narrow range of genres, including poetry, and they themselves declare their aim as that of moving between the text and the social, seeing text as social and social as text. These aims and the reasons for them are even more relevant to the study of Byzantine literature.

How then might literary analysis and social and cultural criticism relate to each other when we try to understand Byzantium? In the Byzantine context, social history has more often than not meant the history of social structures—kinship and family, women (rather than gender), the relations of rich and poor, diet, daily life, material culture—and has involved the collection of material illustrating these lesser-known areas of Byzantine life. It has played a key role in recent attempts to make Byzantium seem more accessible and more "democratic," and to change the direction of research away from elites, or, in art historical terms, from iconography and style, towards material culture and the everyday. The publication series *A People's History of Christianity*, with a volume on Byzantine Christianity, applies the same populist thinking to the field of religion, trying to make it more accessible to modern sensibilities, more "like us."[23]

At the same time a research project based in Vienna that aims to look at the role of ideology in Byzantium in the period from the seventh to the twelfth centuries declares as its focus the lower strata and the common people, and construes ideology as an analytical concept connected with power relations which refers to the whole of society, not simply a society's ruling class. Yet the competitive literary culture of the twelfth-century Constantinopolitan elite also demands interpretation through a broader social and cultural critique.

Comparative history might seem to offer a way forward. However, the economics of production, landholding, taxation and the role of the state, all traditional topics in the history of Byzantium, are where attempts at comparative history have tended to focus, in terms particularly of quantifiable data, which does not help us with the present question. John Haldon's introductory essay in his edited book, *A Social History of Byzantium*, discusses the use of terms like "society," "social system" and "social formation." All are in varying degrees problematic. Haldon advocates a turn towards sociology in Byzantine history, but says that it is not in fact possible to provide a "sociology" of Byzantium. On a closer look it becomes clear that he means an account of Byzantine society in terms of rigorous quantifiable data.[24] This chimes in with recent moves towards writing a broader comparative history, to which Haldon has himself contributed,[25] and which do indeed rely very much on quantitative data. Haldon also espouses the turn in sociological explanation to a neo-Darwinian model, exemplified in the work of the sociologist Gary Runciman;[26] again, the discussion is at a more macro level than our present topic.

However Haldon also says that his aim is to produce "an examination of key facets of Byzantine society in an effort to see what role or function they had"; while he refers to the popular heuristic notion of an imaginative "universe," he locates it firmly in social practice.[27] He goes on to stress the utility of personal and collective narratives in a given society, though at a very theoretical level. He also endorses complexity theory (of which more later), as a way of avoiding the dangers inherent in teleological and causative models of historical explanation.[28] All is however at a high meta-level, with a strong emphasis on the relations between ruling elites and economic issues, but not on cultural or literary production.

While not indeed positivistic (the other major strand in existing discussions), such an approach does not help our present enquiry very much. In particular, culture (another problematic term) is subsumed into social practice. No chapter in Haldon's *Social History of Byzantium* deals with cultural production, literature (despite the emphasis on social narratives) or visual art.

Another discussion from a different point of view, in the context of a chapter by Johann P. Arnason entitled "Byzantium and historical sociology,"[29] is also more about the structures of the Byzantine state than about social history in a micro sense. On the other hand, in her last book, published in 2007, Evelyne Patlagean offered an interpretation of middle and later Byzantium in comparison with western Europe in more traditionally social and indeed anthropological terms, emphasizing family and social relations.[30] Finally, and as already noted, current work on the Palaeologan period is using the methods of complexity theory in a promising way to analyze late Byzantine social structures.[31] Again, however, this is a historical project which in utilizing social network theory—the methodology which, as I mentioned in the Introduction, is being applied to letter collections in the Comnenian period—states that its focus is on statistically analyzable data and available information about social interactions and links. It does not seem to assign agency to literary or cultural factors.

Preiser-Kappeler does allow, if briefly, for the relevance of "the cultural matrix."[32] But we have seen enough to detect a gap between a social history seen primarily in sociological terms and the more literary emphasis in other kinds of scholarship. I would suggest that more is needed to integrate cultural production (I focus here on literature) and social analysis if we are to do justice to the world of Byzantium in the twelfth century. An approach based on discourse analysis is already commonly applied in scholarship on late antique texts and seems to offer a promising way forward for the long twelfth century as well.

Twelfth-century Byzantium saw some new initiatives in education, and a high level of cultural competition, not confined to writers on secular topics. Crucially, it coincided with a period of change in the west that is still the subject of intense debate, and which is sometimes seen as the "birth of a new Europe," or even "the first European revolution," a period that saw the rise of new forms of education, institutionalization and argument.[33] The end of the "long twelfth century" in the west was marked by the Fourth Lateran Council of 1215, and some of the innovations that that century had seen were as contested as anything in the east. While both east and west struggled over the definition of religious orthodoxy, new intellectual developments went much further and had an even wider importance. The culture and the intellectual production of contemporary Byzantium clearly ask for direct comparison with the west.[34] Certainly when seen from the perspective of the surviving and known contemporary dialogues, Comnenian Byzantium was also a world of talk, disagreement and discussion.

The long twelfth century: new approaches to literary production

A better appreciation of Byzantine writing and its aims is finally on the horizon. The concept of intertextuality, preferred in some recent studies to the old concentration on imitation, offers a far more subtle way of reading postclassical and Byzantine texts, and has the great advantage that it also makes it possible to draw on literary approaches used in other cultures.[35] A second major trend lies in the emphasis currently placed on the centrality of performance. Byzantine literary compositions were performed, in the sense of being read aloud to audiences, probably small and certainly socially selective.[36] The exact nature and composition of these gatherings, circles or salons is less clear, as is the question of whether such performances extended to every kind of literary text. But patronage was very important to the writers and intellectuals who were connected with—or hoped to be connected with —the teaching establishments and aristocratic households of contemporary Constantinople. The very nature of this "rhetorical theatre," to borrow a term from Magdalino, also affected the style and tone of what was written and performed. Audiences looked for and appreciated drama, display and learning—what we might call rhetorical bravura. This aspect of twelfth-century society was both a product of and a determinant of its characteristic literary expression.

It was also a highly self-conscious society, and performance can be understood in a different way; for instance Anthony Kaldellis uses the term "the performance of Hellenism," as part of the title of his discussion of twelfth-century literature.[37] I shall have more to say on this later.

Some scholars, including Kaldellis himself, also apply the term "Third Sophistic" to this period, suggesting similarities with the Second Sophistic movement of the early Roman empire; indeed, some twelfth-century Byzantines had the literary productions of that period in mind when they wrote themselves. The analogy is appealing, even though the same term has also been applied to other periods, for instance to the Greek literature of the late antique period,[38] or as the "late Byzantine sophistic" claimed by Niels Gaul for the Palaeologan period.[39] Caution is therefore needed. In order to make the analogy with the Second Sophistic work fully for the twelfth century, we need more direct comparison between the twelfth-century situation and the social circumstances and activity of "sophists" in the Second Sophistic. Sophists in the early empire were real performers, practising voice control and projection and mannerisms of delivery. Less is known so far in the Comnenian period than for the early empire about the actual circumstances of performance and presentation, or indeed reception, though hostile accounts talk disparagingly about the same striving for fame and effect as in the earlier context. Yet here again comparison between the literary world of twelfth-century Byzantium and the Greek literary world of late antiquity or the early empire offers many fruitful lines of enquiry, and given the currently emerging focus on the postclassical this is likely to develop further.

Less useful is the tendency to look at twelfth-century literature as a kind of renaissance—but renaissance of what? Or is it being claimed that it was a precursor of "the" Renaissance? Margaret Alexiou has written of "a new literary consciousness in Constantinopolitan intellectual circles, comparable with, yet significantly different from, developments in the west, sometimes anticipating the Renaissance" and connected with a "consolidation" of the "socio-economic expansion which began under Alexius I."[40] But again, such a "twelfth-century renaissance" is only one of several such "renaissances" detected at different times in the history of Byzantium. One of these may be more convincing than another, but all are premised on the vulnerable assumption that rather than having its own autonomy Byzantine culture was primarily about classical "revivals."

Of course the idea of a renaissance may also be about more than cultural revival. Strikingly, in 1993 Paul Magdalino concluded one of the longest and most detailed historical discussions of whether or not there was a twelfth-century renaissance in Byzantium, by arguing that Byzantium failed. It did not "create mental systems from first principles;" it suffered from a "loss of intellectual nerve"; it lacked intellectual specialization; and in comparison with the contemporary west it was "inward-looking rather than expansionist." On this view, cultural change in Byzantium was "not spontaneous," but rather a "patriotic response to the jolt of confrontation, or invasion by, a more dynamic culture." Earlier in the same discussion we read that Byzantium in the period suffered a "failure of cultural nerve" that "prevented the Orthodoxy of New Rome from matching the cultural achievements of Roman Catholicism."[41] That is, without the impact of the west, no cultural change in Byzantium. When it did come, it was "esoteric" and "myopic"; Byzantium lacked an infrastructure of legalism, scholasticism or commercialism, only "a visceral and cerebral Orthodoxy."[42]

Such dismal judgements about Byzantine culture in the twelfth century take one by surprise by their vehemence. Clearly religion constitutes a central interpretative problem for Byzantinists; it affects literary production just as much as any other sphere, and it is an issue that I will be addressing in these chapters. I will challenge the idea that Byzantine Orthodoxy was fixed and unchanging, but I also want to argue for a more integrated view of Byzantine culture, bringing together the religious and the secular—an aim that, I will argue, a fuller recognition of the use of the dialogue form in the period can help us to achieve.

Why the emphasis on rhetoric?

The works and writers I discuss here belong to high-class circles and to a culture in which the practice of rhetoric was enormously important.[43] Members of this literary elite drew on and used a large body of rhetorical theory, albeit one in which guidance on the writing of dialogue hardly featured; and in many cases the same persons both taught rhetoric and practised it. Writers in this tradition valued learning and aspired to give their works a highly sophisticated veneer, including for the most part a specially artificial linguistic register,[44] or "sociolect." The twelfth century is also the period when we have the first literary works deliberately composed in the so-called vernacular, itself a form of sociolect.[45] However the high-style productions had another powerful role over and beyond their narrowly literary or rhetorical aspects. To cite one recent contribution dealing with the period from the ninth to the end of the twelfth centuries, "rhetoricians are central to the creation of a Constantinopolitan high orthodox as well as Hellenic culture that was utilized both for the ideological export needs of the Byzantine state and for interior consumption, as a cultural capital indispensable for social advancement."[46] This was a period high in internal and external tensions, in which it would be a mistake to imagine that any single orthodox or Hellenic culture was produced. Yet such an emphasis on the agency of these discursive practices within twelfth-century Byzantine society chimes well with the argument I want to make here.

Dialogues in the long twelfth century

It is a nice thought that Natalie Zemon Davis's book *Women on the Margins* is prefaced by an imaginary dialogue between the three women, a Jew, a Catholic and a Protestant, who are her subjects, with Natalie herself as the author—their interviewer—and that she writes about the uses of dialogue in her opening pages.[47]

Twelfth-century literary dialogues in Byzantium follow in a long tradition that has not yet been fully explored. They also vary considerably, from highly polished compositions to what seem to be more utilitarian exchanges verging on the related genre of questions and answers or *erotapokriseis*, which has recently been the subject of two volumes of collected studies.[48] As I remarked earlier, some of the dialogues that relate to actual contemporary debates, especially on religious matters, have been viewed as a form of "rhetorical journalism,"[49] although at times their authors also explicitly justify the choice of dialogue as a form particularly suited to philosophical or theological discussion. Clearly writing in the form of a dialogue has an abiding appeal in itself, even in our own day. It allows for a narrative setting and for characterization, and it can work well as a means of expressing or exploring a range of views while leaving options open. Yet while literary dialogues can be dialogic, not all are, certainly in the religious and philosophical spheres. We shall explore this further in relation to twelfth-century Byzantium in chapters two and three. But secular literary or "satirical" dialogues may also have agendas, as we shall also see.

37

Some dialogues composed in eleventh and twelfth-century Byzantium have indeed featured in discussions of the literature of the period. Chief among them is the anonymous dialogue known as the *Timarion*, recounting an enforced journey to Hades; here the dialogue part is mainly a frame for narrative, and the character called Timarion tells his story at length, though punctuated by brief questions and observations by Kydion.[50] (This framing is not unique: an author known as "Philip the philosopher," seemingly of the twelfth century, also cast his essay on Heliodorus within the frame of a dialogue, with debts to the pseudo-Platonic *Axiochus*.)[51] The *Timarion* is usually classed with the group of "satirical" dialogues more or less in the manner of Lucian, and is transmitted together with Lucian's works.[52] However, its tone and purpose have puzzled scholars: is it a bitter or a "harmless" satire, a "playful, lighthearted commentary" (as seen by most recent critics, according to Dimitris Krallis), a comic dialogue or a "literary, satirical and philosophical narrative"—all terms recently applied to it?[53] In a recent contribution Anthony Kaldellis refers both to a mix of genres and to Lucianic satire, while claiming that at its likely date, c. 1100, Lucian was not yet commonly enough imitated in Byzantium for one to be able to speak of a genre of Lucianic dialogue. Later in the same article he allows without further comment for dialogue and dialogic interplay within the *Timarion*.[54] Dimitris Krallis is less certain, seeing the work as a dialogue "at first sight only in a superficial form," but also pointing out the dialogue section further on in the text between Timarion and his teacher, the leading intellectual Theodore of Smyrna. Yet while the *Timarion* is anything but straightforward, its literary framing as a dialogue and the exchanges that take place in its imaginary Hades bring it well within our purview here.

As he tells Kydion, the hero Timarion had set off to attend the feast of St Demetrius in Thessalonike, but became ill on his way back and was seized and carried down to the Underworld by two demons. There he met not only an array of classical figures—Minos, Aesculapius, Hippocrates, Erasistratus, Diogenes, Aristarchus and Phrynichus—but also the ninth-century emperor Theophilus, the famous eleventh-century rhetor and philosopher Michael Psellus, and John Italus, the subject of a notorious heresy trial under Alexius I. One of the central figures among them is Theodore of Smyrna, who succeeded John Italus in his teaching post, and was cleverer than Italus at managing his career. He is presented as a devotee of the orators of the Second Sophistic, praised for his declamations, his brilliant lectures and resonant delivery and made to talk of how successful he had been and how much he had earned.[55] The work is full of Homeric and Euripidean allusions. Yet the rivalry between paganism and Christianity is also a key theme. Theodore observes, "the religion of the Galilaeans has spread over all the world." In a court case in which Timarion accuses the two demons of improperly capturing him, the judges are the unlikely mix of Aeacus, Minos and the Emperor Theophilus. Theodore is counsel for Timarion and his speech is so eloquent that "the Christians" shout, jump for joy and congratulate him. Of course Timarion wins; the verdict is read out by Psellus as clerk of the court, and Timarion is enabled to make his exit and tell his tale.

There is clearly more going on here than is immediately obvious. As Timarion makes his way up to earth, his mentor Theodore wrily comments: "It's a long time since anyone was resurrected." The treatment of John Italus is also curious. He is said to have "put on the mantle of the Galilaeans," which he refuses to take off, and is accordingly stoned by the "dialecticians," whereupon he exclaims "Aristotle, Aristotle, O syllogism, O sophism, where are you now that I need you?"[56] It is hardly surprising that the *Timarion* was later criticized for treating Christianity with disrespect; at the same time, its themes and characters root it in broader twelfth-century intellectual controversies. As Eustratius of Nicaea found, to be accused of relying on Aristotelian syllogisms could be dangerous, even though in practice, as we shall see, syllogisms were regularly employed as a mode of argument by both Byzantines and Latins.

Not only do Christianity and Aristotelianism feature in the dialogue but also the rival merits of rhetoric. Having observed what happened to John Italus, Theodore of Smyrna knew how to survive. After Timarion tells him how John Italus had been routed, and how Psellus had been greeted with enthusiasm by the "sophists," Kydion asks how Timarion's "own Smyrnite sophist" Theodore had fared. Timarion replies:

> "Well, Kydion, as I was about to say, he kept himself largely aloof from those sharp-witted leaders of the philosophical sects, except when he needed to ask a question or request clarification concerning a particular theory. But he got on like a house on fire with the rhetoricians, especially Polemo and Herodes and Aristides [leading lights of the Second Sophistic]." (*Timarion*, 45, trans. Baldwin, 74)

The same Theodore also wrote a commentary on Aristotle and a work on the theological differences with the Latins: such were the complexities of twelfth-century intellectual culture.

The *Timarion* has sometimes been attributed to the leading poet and intellectual Theodore Prodromos, author of *Rhodanthe and Dosikles*, one of the high-style romances produced in the twelfth century, as well as of several dialogues in both prose and verse, among them the *Xenedemos*, the *Amarantos* (a *jeu d'esprit* dealing with the philosophy of Epicureanism), and the *Bion prasis*, about an imaginary sale of classical celebrities, a work recently described as belonging "on the top-ten list of most undervalued Byzantine texts."[57] But even if the *Timarion*'s authorship remains uncertain it acts as a window into the world of twelfth-century schools and the students who gathered around some of the leading figures of the period, and gives us a feel not only for a less black and white view of religious allegiance than usual, but also for current rivalries based on the respective merits of rhetoric and philosophy and the uncertain division between them. Commentaries on Aristotle were a feature of the period,[58] and the theological dialogues that we will consider in chapter two were often accompanied by long lists of syllogisms. The *Timarion* may be a dialogue only in part, but it conveys contemporary intellectual as well as literary concerns and the tensions and the to and fro of argument among the *literati* and their followers.

Prodromos's *Xenedemos*, or *Voices*, also deals with philosophical themes, including the hot topic of the day, the reception of Plato and Aristotle among twelfth-century intellectuals. Its format is familiar within the corpus of late antique and Byzantine dialogues:[59] it consists of an opening, in which an Athenian called Musaios comes to Constantinople to find out about a great philosopher called Theocles of whom he has heard, a framing dialogue in which Musaios questions Xenedemos about Theocles, and then a recounted or indirect dialogue in which Xenedemos describes being questioned by Theocles when he was a young man. Theocles expounds Aristotle's *Categories* on qualities, and exposes Xenedemos's confidence in Porphyry's *Isagoge*, the commonly used introduction to the *Categories*. The dialogue also frequently cites Plato, and possibly underlying the representation of Theocles is Prodromos's real friend Michael Italicus, teacher in Constantinople and disciple of Psellus, with whom he corresponded.[60] Prodromos was an advocate of Plato himself,[61] but as with adhesion to both rhetoric and philosophy, enthusiasm for Plato and Aristotle often co-existed in these circles. Like the *Timarion,* but in more dialogic mode, the *Xenedemos* allows yet another glimpse into these complexities and tensions.

Prodromos was a highly visible twelfth-century intellectual and an immensely versatile writer in a range of different genres and registers.[62] Although like many others he ended his life as a monk, this had not stopped him from composing broadly satirical works and dialogues. Another dialogue, the *Bion prasis* (*"Sale of Lives"*), imagines a sale by Zeus and Hermes of a group of classical characters—Homer, Hippocrates, Euripides, Aristophanes, Pomponius (a second-century Roman lawyer, who speaks in Latin, so that a prospective buyer needs Hermes to interpret for him), and Demosthenes. However, as Marciniak argues, the work is humorous rather than satirical, and like the *Timarion*, its connection to Lucian's dialogue with the same title is in fact rather loose. It is thus over-simplifying merely to label the dialogue Lucianic without further exploration.[63] Marciniak sees it as partly a cento and suggests that it was written to be appreciated by Prodromos's students, who would enjoy its humour and its cleverness. If correct this does not of course reduce its literary value, or rule out its also having been read or performed in a *theatron*.[64]

There was certainly an element of rhetorical display in these compositions, and indeed in Prodromos's other dialogues too. The *Katomyomachia*, or "War between the cat and the mice," written in iambics and more like a play than a dialogue, draws on Homer and on Aeschylus's *Persians*.[65] The *Amarantos* combines philosophical discussion with a dramatic interruption;[66] here the main characters are from Athens. Hermocles arrives late for a meeting with two friends,

Diophantos and Philolaos, who are followers of Democritus. Hermocles is a follower of Epicurus and they debate the merits or otherwise of the two philosophers, until Amarantos arrives. Refusing to act as the judge, he tells the others instead about a wedding he has attended in which an old bachelor has suddenly married a young girl. Following Platonic precedent, the dialogue is named after one of its characters, who reports the story. Here again the allusion to Lucian is distant, and a closer look reveals that Prodromos is taking the opportunity to explore and play with current philosophical and theological issues and themes in which he was himself concerned.[67]

Overall, Prodromos allows us to see the many possibilities of the dialogue form, ranging from the comic to the serious. Real contemporary issues, philosophical and intellectual, are addressed, even if indirectly and in a literary dress. Read attentively, in fact, these dialogues reveal that twelfth-century Constantinople was a complex place, full of tensions and argument.

Some other examples will underline the point. Puzzling as it may seem to modern critics, Theophylact of Ohrid, one of the leading churchmen of the eleventh and early twelfth centuries, famously also wrote a defence of eunuchs sometime in the reign of Alexius I, and cast it in the form of a dialogue. It consists of a reported dialogue, with speeches for and against, with a transition between them, preceded by two prologues, one in verse and one in prose, naming the personages, setting the scene in Thessalonike and addressing the work to Theophylact's "brother" Demetrius, himself a eunuch. The writer says he is reporting a discussion he heard in Thessalonike between a cleric and a pious eunuch whose nephew was about to be made a eunuch too; it is not clear why the setting is Thessalonike, and the body of the work is devoid of any further realistic touches. Nor is it entirely clear whether the "brother" is Theophylact's real brother or not. Margaret Mullett calls the work a disputation rather than a dialogue.[68] However given the sheer variety of form in Byzantine dialogues, which is yet to be studied, and to avoid misleading western connotations, it seems to me that it would be better to avoid the term disputation in a Byzantine context: some Byzantine dialogues relied more on long speeches than the interplay of speakers, but they lacked the technical features of disputation as developed in western scholasticism. On the face of it, Theophylact's work defends the eunuch state against its detractors. Yet many things about it remain unclear. A recent detailed study by Charis Messis sees a range of key contemporary concerns in what at first sight seems to be a rather strange work.[69] On this reading, rather than being a piece of biography, however artificial, it reflects concerns about trends in contemporary monasticism, while its otherwise strange and negative section on the Emperor Justinian may constitute a warning to Alexius I; moreover, some of the opinions expressed set Theophylact at odds with positions taken in another work with which we shall be concerned later, the *Dogmatic Panoply* of Zigabenus. These brief remarks fail to do justice to a complex argument, but it is worth noting that Messis connects the work with Theophylact's closeness to the circle of the Empress Anna Dalassena, the mother of the Emperor Alexius, and places it in the context of the controversy about church treasures with which this chapter opened. What seems on first sight to be a classic dialogic treatment of a contemporary issue turns out yet again to reflect a complex context of wider contemporary disagreements and arguments.

Current discussions of Comnenian literature tend to deal with the secular, or "satirical," dialogues in high-style Greek, but not with the theological (and indeed with a limited range of the former).[70] Paul Magdalino complains that the theological dialogues are "derivative in the extreme," and that the dogmatic armouries considered further below rely on "potted argument." All in all, he says, "theology, it seems, was not allowed to share in the cultural expansion of the age."[71] We must not of course fall into the trap of claiming implausible literary merit for particular works, but I will argue here and in what follows against such an artificial distinction.

The interplay of ecclesiastical and lay is in fact one of the key features of the period. I began with the case of Eustratius of Nicaea, who chose to couch his refutation of Leo of Chalcedon in the form of a Platonic dialogue. Another early example in the period is the so-called *Dioptra* of Philip Monotropos, a dialogue in not very elevated verse between body and soul, following in a long tradition of works on that theme.[72] We have already discussed the defence of eunuchs by Theophylact of Ohrid, and I will be considering the reports of debates with the Latins in the next chapters and those with or against Jews and Muslims in the third. But religious dialogues were not confined to these subjects. The dialogue *On Demons* attributed to Psellus, but perhaps rather from the twelfth century, has a certain Timotheus reporting a discussion about demonology between a man from Thrace and a monk who had formerly been a Bogomil.[73] Doctrinal arguments under Manuel I produced several works in dialogue form, including the Emperor Manuel's discussion with the patriarch Nicholas Mouzalon about his election (below). Other dialogues on theological topics included the emperor's discussions about the Armenians with Michael III Anchialos, who was both patriarch and consul of the philosophers, and the records of two sets of discussions by Manuel's representative Theorianos, also with the Armenians and discussed in chapter two. Theorianos was a layman, but was nevertheless able to deploy the full range of theological arguments on the religious differences between the Greek and Armenian churches. The same was also true of Andronikos Kamateros, author of the massive *Sacred Arsenal,* also of the early 1170s, which dealt with differences with the Latins, the Armenians and others.[74]

Did Eustratius write his refutation of the arguments of Leo of Chalcedon in the form of a dialogue because he thought this nod to Plato would make his case more acceptable to the highly placed members of the court who had been persuaded by Leo, and because he thought it would impress them? Later in our period, when the Emperor Manuel discovered an irregularity in the recent election of Nicholas Mouzalon as patriarch, a two-day debate was held between emperor and patriarch of which a record survives.[75] In a familiar move in such arguments, Manuel accuses Mouzalon of sophistry, while himself employing the techniques of dialectic. No surprise that Mouzalon stepped down. A doctrinal dispute then began as to whether the sacrifice in the Eucharist was offered only to the Father or to both the Father and the Son. Again the arguments were put in the form of a Platonizing dialogue with pretensions to high style, this

49

time by Soterichos Panteugenos, the patriarch-elect of Antioch,[76] to which a reply was composed by Nicholas of Methone, and which Soterichos circulated by himself for effect. The emperor summoned a synod, and took part in the debate; Soterichos refused to recant or to appear for the verdict, but was deposed anyway.[77] This is another example both of imperial pressure and of resistance, and again a Platonizing dialogue was felt to be a suitable mode of communication. The work and its arguments were taken seriously, even if Manuel's position prevailed, and the eventual deposition of Soterichos was far from straightforward. As we shall see in chapter two, the emperor took a very active role in such matters, and again engaged in dialogue himself when he debated with the patriarch Michael III Anchialos about the Armenians and with the Roman cardinals on the differences between the Latins and Greeks, as reported in the *Sacred Arsenal* of Andronikos Kamateros.

"Religious" and "secular"'

The crossover that we find in this period between secular literary works and theological or religious writing is intriguing. Can it tell us something about Byzantium that is so far not being captured? Like scholars of the early empire and even of late antiquity,[78] many students of Byzantium have a problem with theology while yet others limit themselves to it; still more separate their subject matter into two different spheres, or relegate theological and religious writing to the history of the church. Yet another problem concerns the relation of philosophy and theology, traditionally seen as being almost coterminous in Byzantium; this too is relevant for anyone attempting to understand our dialogues. Paul Lemerle wrote of "le gouvernement des philosophes" in the eleventh century,[79] and philosophy remained important in our period, though, as we saw, it could also render its proponents open to attack. The evaluation of Byzantine philosophy is another work in progress and current scholars are reclaiming it as a genuinely autonomous field,[80] though the issues are far from clear as yet. At least we can now say that even the more literary of the twelfth-century dialogues so far mentioned reveal tensions both between rhetoric and philosophy and between philosophical and theological issues.

In intellectual and religious matters the Comnenian period is particularly challenging. Controversy still rages as to whether it was "repressive" (as suggested by some of the actions of Alexius I, including the trials for wrong belief held during his reign, the sponsorship under Alexius and Manuel I of doctrinal com-

51

pilations, and their several proclamations about correct belief).[81] An article published in 1975 by Robert Browning is still central to this "repressive" interpretation, and even now remains the starting point for many other discussions.[82] Against this view is set the flourishing of literary creativity and intellectual productivity in the same period. Paul Magdalino has argued that "repression" was not in fact very thoroughgoing, and more recently for a development from repression towards self-expression, humanism and secular criticism, but his discussion in his book on *The Empire of Manuel I Komnenos* echoes the language of Browning's concluding paragraph.

The place of religion in Byzantium needs better analysis. The problem with the striking term "the guardians of Orthodoxy" used by Magdalino, and argued by him to extend effectively to all the top echelons of society, including lay intellectuals, is that it assumes that orthodoxy was a given. As I have argued elsewhere, and as is clear from the efforts to which Alexius and Manuel I went in our period, this was very far from the case.[83] No matter how much its continuity and its God-given nature were proclaimed, Byzantine orthodoxy was constantly challenged. The twelfth century offers an instructive example, with its heresy processes, its denunciations of heresy and its voluminous declarations of orthodox belief. A large body of scholarship on the early Christian centuries and late antiquity has now shown how both orthodoxy and "heresy" were constructed, not given, and it would be a mistake to assume that this did not continue in Byzantium. As his daughter Anna tells us, the Emperor Alexius presented himself as the custodian and enforcer of orthodoxy; so too did his grandson Manuel I. In so doing they issued their own documents and stimulated many works by others. We need to remember that this zeal for defining orthodoxy was manifested in a context where reaching agreement with others—especially Latins and Armenians but also Paulicians and even Muslims—was a practical as well as a doctrinal aim. The long twelfth century also saw an important reform edict issued by Alexius I,[84] and several major internal disputes on doctrinal matters, starting from the renewed arguments about religious images with which I began. In the reign of Manuel I the issue moved to the nature of the Eucharistic elements, the sacrifice of Christ and the interpretation of the verse "The Father is greater than I" (John 14:28). In 1166 this also produced a weighty imperial edict, for Manuel needed internal as well as external agreement.[85] All these arguments involved the direct participation of the emperor, and in his preface Kamateros referred to the state of the church in Manuel's reign as "dreadfully storm-tossed."[86] These episodes also produced torrents of words, some of them presented in the form of dialogues. At the very least, the sociology of the period ought to include the question of how texts such as these construct power structures and how they formed social opinion.[87]

We ought to be on the alert in other ways too. As I have already said, orthodoxy was not agreed and settled. Agreeing what was and was not orthodox was as much a competitive activity as anything that went on in the literary salons or round the court. Often enough the same individuals were involved—as for example the historian, letter-writer and rhetorician Niketas Choniates at the end of our period, who also compiled a massive compendium of orthodoxy, the *Dogmatic Panoply* or "*Treasury*." This enormous work has still not been fully edited, while the earlier twelfth-century *Sacred Arsenal*, composed by Andronikos Kamateros, a very well-born high official and member of the court (Manuel's "justice minister") in the early 1170s, has only now received a critical edition, and then only of the first part.[88] Even earlier, but still in our period, another such work, also a *Dogmatic Panoply*, was composed for Alexius I by Euthymius Zigabenus.[89] The fact that its author was a monk should not lead us to relegate it to some special theological closet. In fact the contemporary significance attached to these works is shown by the fact that prestigious display manuscripts were produced for both the *Dogmatic Panoply* and the *Sacred Arsenal*, with illustrations and dedicatory verses; one of the epigrams in the well-known poetry collection contained in Codex Marcianus graecus 524 (no. 331) is closely related to the verses of George Skylitzes which introduce the *Sacred Arsenal*.[90] These are not the mere tedious compilations they may appear to modern eyes. Like the collections of patristic *florilegia* (proof texts from the Fathers) which are integral to them, and which had been a feature of theological writing since late antiquity, they were written with a purpose, namely to define, assert and display, in fact to perform, the particular "orthodox" line of the moment. The very fact that a number of individuals who seemed to pose religious threats, such as Leo of Chalcedon, Eustratius of Nicaea, John Italus, Basil the Bogomil, Soterichos Panteugenos and others, were tried and sanctioned is enough to show that these issues and the way that they were expressed really mattered.

The kind of constructivist approach that I am suggesting would seem routine in scholarship on other periods,[91] and it can surely be useful for Byzantium. It may be most obviously applicable in the field of theological writing, but it should not be confined to that. Might we also be able to look at the broader body of elite writing from the period in such terms?

Conclusion

My contention here is that to separate theological from secular works is a mistake. Indeed, the type of writing on which I want to focus—namely dialogues—embraces both spheres in a particularly dramatic way.

There are many excellent studies of individual literary works from the Comnenian period—even though dialogues are still the poor relation—and some scholars are already incorporating a sociological approach in their studies of eleventh- and twelfth-century literature, even if these studies are limited to certain kinds of writing. But while it is easy enough to see that the twelfth century was a time of intense cultural and intellectual ferment, its literature has yet to be viewed in a genuinely inclusive context.

My aim is to propound a unified view of religious/theological and secular writing in twelfth-century Byzantium, one that does not simply ask who the audience was or why people wrote, but also how all these literary productions combined with other contemporary expressions to produce what Pierre Bourdieu called the *habitus*, the characteristic structural systems of the place and period.[92] One might indeed appeal to Michel Foucault and use the term "power," were it not that its utility has been diminished through overuse. If in this particular period it becomes clear that the *habitus* was in construction or under challenge, that is an important outcome. One study of ideology in Byzantium points to the need to include Byzantine philosophy as well as religious and theological discourse,[93] and Bourdieu's analysis of social markers in *Distinction* and of the academic profession in *Homo Academicus* also seems obviously relevant to the culture I have been describing in Byzantium.[94] But the point I would like to make here is about literary production itself, namely to argue that these literary works had their own agency in terms of creating cultural and social change. I focus on literature, in which I include dialogues and many other theological works usually consigned to specialist tomes where they can be safely ignored, but the argument could also be applied to other spheres of expression. If, as I said, what we actually find is continuing tension or even conflict, then that will also be useful in helping to understand the dynamics of Byzantine society in the twelfth century.[95]

The "arguing it out" that took place in the dialogues of twelfth-century Byzantium can thus stand for the stresses in contemporary Byzantine society, and this will become the clearer if we take the totality of literary production rather than only part of it.

In the next chapter I will explore the question of whether such an approach can also help with the body of literature arising from the debates and discussions between Latins and Byzantines on such matters as the *Filioque*, the use of azymes (unleavened bread) in the Eucharist, or the primacy of the papacy. These texts, usually left to theologians, or in some cases to western medievalists, are rarely differentiated in the detail they actually deserve. The discussion will then also enable us to approach the question of what comparison can be made between Byzantium and the twelfth-century west, and how far the experience of westerners and exposure to western developments impacted on the Greek east. This is one part of the need being increasingly advocated by scholars to relocate our conception of Byzantium in a global or at least transnational context. Equally it is basic to the evaluation of Byzantine culture itself. My second and third chapters will approach this broader question in different ways, again by foregrounding the dialogue and debate texts, which, as I will argue, have much more to tell us than has so far been realised.

Chapter 2

Latins and Greeks

To quote from John Haldon, "It is clear that the [Byzantine] empire's internal history can only be understood in its international context."[1] This chapter will raise the very basic question of the place of Byzantium, and of what has been labelled "Orthodox culture" (not the "Orthodox civilization" of recent geopolitical generalizations, but specifically the culture of Byzantium itself) in its key position between west and east in the medieval period. It also takes us further into the territory of how historians of culture and society deal with religion, and, in the particular case of Byzantium, with the theological issues that seem abstruse and irrelevant to many today.

In this chapter I will direct the argument to the debates between "Latins" and "Greeks," or to be more precise, between Catholics and Orthodox, with a diversion into the dialogues between Byzantines and Armenians, while in chapter three I will focus on Byzantine writing about Jews and Muslims in the long twelfth century as reflected in dialogue texts.

We might start, however, with a deeper question about the identity of Byzantium itself. Garth Fowden's latest book, *Before and After Muhammad*,[2] asserts the claim that late antiquity continued up to the year AD 1000, the end of the first millennium. However in this scenario, the intellectual energies and spirit of philosophical enquiry had already passed to the east, from sixth-century Alexandria, through Syria, to the world of Abbasid Baghdad. That much is not new. The story has often been told before, though indeed some of its outlines have recently been challenged. But in this familiar eastward narrative of intellectual transmission now endorsed again by Fowden (with a nod to the equally familiar "Christian European" and western narrative of development stretching in a line from antiquity to the late medieval period), Byzantium is left out. Worse, it is singled out for comment on its lack of intellectual power and its allegedly "low-level" theological competence.[3] Fowden's is indeed a late antique historian's book. Had its scope been extended further than the end of the first millennium, into the period that is my main concern here, the author's attitude could not have been so dismissive. But perhaps we can use this example as some indication of a much wider phenomenon—the tendency either to address Byzantium in isolation, or conversely, effectively to leave it out altogether in historical accounts that claim to take the broader global perspective. It is also noticeable that Byzantium still plays only a minor part in the growing amount of comparative history in the ancient and medieval periods.[4]

The facts were very different. Byzantium was already part of a world that went far beyond the Mediterranean, but with the advent of the Crusades, the long twelfth century saw Byzantium caught in new and urgent ways between the demands of the west and those of the east. From the later twelfth century, and especially after 1204, when the Byzantine court was driven from Constantinople and the single empire replaced by several small polities each claiming to be a Byzantine successor state, the Mediterranean world also became more fragmented. Historians must therefore perforce take a broader and more global approach.[5] But already before that Byzantium was linked in to Mediterranean and other zones of trading, travel and cultural interaction. Even if my focus here is less expansive, we will still need to have in mind these broader cross-cultural themes.

Some of the scholarship on the literary production discussed above already envisages a cultural impact from the west;[6] as I mentioned earlier, it has been argued that the high-style Greek romances of the twelfth century for instance were indebted to contemporary Latin romance. However the comparison is not always made in a flattering way. For instance, for Magdalino, the outpouring of literary activity in twelfth-century Byzantium would not have happened without the stimulus (or as he puts it, the "jolt") of the west;[7] moreover, it failed even before the disaster of the Fourth Crusade in 1204, because of its "obsessive" features, linked closely in the author's mind with its religious culture.

Can more be done, then, with the apparently unpromising subject of religious debate with Latins in the long twelfth century? (I prefer to avoid the commonly used term "polemic," because it assumes a purpose in the texts that is not always there and which I believe needs to be argued for case by case.)

Developments in the west

The eleventh and twelfth centuries saw great changes in western Europe in terms of intellectual and religious developments. Importantly for my present subject, they included the rise of disputation as a key activity in the new schools and universities that grew up in western Europe. A broad literary form that had been employed since classical antiquity for philosophical discussion and for a variety of literary uses, as well as in theological argument from the theoretical to the discussions in church councils, now acquired a whole new technical meaning and utility. In addition to these social developments, scholars and theologians frequently chose to compose their works in dialogue form. However, the context in the Latin west was very different from that of twelfth-century Byzantium. One difference lay in the geographical spread within which these developments took place; instead of being concentrated in the capital, Latin schools were spread, and schoolmen travelled over a wide area of western Europe, including Canterbury in England. One can see some broad similarities with contemporary educational developments within Constantinople, but also some sharp differences. In the west, in particular, multiple centres of education were attached to the great monasteries and abbeys like the eleventh-century abbeys of Bec in Normandy or St Victor in Paris, or grew up round cathedrals, as at Laon, Notre Dame, Reims and Chartres; teachers like Abelard attracted groups of followers, and individual scholars could and did move their activities from one school to another.[8] As in Byzantium, there were competitions between schools and between individuals, but in contrast with the situation in Byzantium, where Aristotle did not need to be rediscovered, the translation of Aristotle's logical works into Latin in the twelfth century gave a powerful impetus towards the evolution of a more formal disputation procedure. According to Alex Novikoff, over eighty dialogues were written in Latin from the 1080s to the end of the twelfth century.[9] Anselm of Bec, later of Canterbury, was a central figure in this development and wrote at least seven dialogues himself on theological subjects; his example was followed by his disciples Gilbert Crispin and Honorius Augustodunensis. Dialogues were also composed against Jews, for instance by the same Gilbert Crispin (who became abbot of Westminster), by Peter Abelard and by Peter the Venerable, and we shall encounter some of these in chapter three. As was the case in Byzantium, dialogues had been composed, if in fewer numbers, before the eleventh century,[10] but a strikingly new culture of dialogue and disputation came into being from the mid-eleventh century. It is worth pointing out, with Novikoff,[11] that in the west, in contrast with the Greek east, even if we allow that direct acquaintance with Plato's dialogues was selective at best in Byzantium, most of Plato's dialogues still remained unknown. For men like Anselm, Aristotle presented a closer model both for dialogue and for syllogistic reasoning.

In the same period the papal reforms took the western church in new directions. From the end of the eleventh century the advent of the Crusades also brought more westerners to Constantinople and thus new exposure between Latins and Greeks. The so-called schism, or at least the differences in practice and ideology between the eastern and western churches, now acquired more urgency as both sides were forced to reassess their positions.[12] With the adoption of clerical celibacy in the west they also acquired a new topic. Finally, also during this period, the west gradually became a "persecuting society," in the well-known words of R. I. Moore,[13] a term that has been taken up and applied to Byzantium as well.[14]

At first sight some of these developments also seem recognizable in contemporary Byzantium. For instance, intensified controls on marriage;[15] elements of ecclesiastical "reform"; high-profile condemnation of heretics; and a prescriptive literature, both moral and doctrinal. Add to that an inherited anti-heretical literature that had been in place continuously since the very early Christian period and that aimed at demonizing "heretical" doctrines and groups. The new and confident configuration of the papacy was also a factor to be reckoned with. I will leave aside for the moment the question of how far these comparisons can take us, but we can at least agree that Byzantium cannot be understood in isolation.

Relations between Byzantium and the west were not merely about religious differences or about the particular circumstances surrounding the Crusades. Italian trading cities like Amalfi extended their influence in the eleventh century, as did Venice, the first to be granted a concession within Constantinople, while the loss of Bari to the Normans in 1071 transformed the dynamics of southern Italy and heralded a new threat to Byzantium. Trading links could give rise to mounting tensions: Venetian ships received customs benefits from Alexius I, but Venice reacted badly when these were withdrawn under his son and successor John II Comnenus, a move followed by much stronger measures under Manuel I, an emperor who was in general pro-Latin on religious issues. Within Constantinople, tensions rose and such was the strength of anti-Latin feeling in the later twelfth century that soon after Manuel's death in 1180 Latins were the subject of a massacre in the city. Finally, as is well known, the Fourth Crusade which turned on Constantinople in 1204 was led by the Venetians themselves, under their aged Doge Enrico Dandolo.

Such was the background for the various visits to Constantinople by ecclesiastics from the west during our period, and for the public discussions with Byzantine representatives that took place on those occasions. These debates, or some of them at least, have been studied, but the extent of scholarly work that has been done on them is very uneven, especially in terms of the editing of texts. They have largely been left to theologians and historians of the church, rather than fully incorporated into the broader cultural history of the period, let alone into the intellectual and literary production of the day. They are for instance routinely omitted from the large amount of scholarship on literary production in the period. The excellent survey from 1992 by Ruth Macrides and Paul Magdalino dealing with Byzantine rhetoric in the period, selects some seventeen individual writers for discussion, but evidently considers these inter-religious debates as falling outside its brief.[16] I have already mentioned some of the debates and the dialogues that were written on internal theological or doctrinal matters; in contrast the evidence for Christian-Jewish and Christian-Muslim debate will be my subject in chapter three. Manuel I's eagerness to secure doctrinal union in the 1160s and 1170s also led to correspondence and meetings with the Armenians, which I will discuss below. But the twelfth century saw a number of important discussions, with their purported records, between Latins and Greeks, and these now deserve a closer look.

Panoplies and Arsenals:
arming oneself against heresy

We should begin with the vast compendium against heresy (that is, anything others believe) and statement of orthodoxy (what we believe ourselves) commissioned by the Emperor Alexius I Comnenus in the context of the trial and condemnation of the Bogomil leader Basil, as recounted by Anna Comnena in what is in fact one of the stranger and more fanciful episodes in her history.[17] This was the immensely long *Dogmatic Panoply*, or "armament for doctrine," compiled by Euthymius Zigabenus, which followed a tradition exemplified most spectacularly by Epiphanius of Salamis in his fifth-century *Panarion*, or "medicine-chest" against heresy, and continued by others including John of Damascus. According to Anna, Alexius commissioned Zigabenus to write a refutation of Bogomilism, and to do so in the context of a refutation of all heresies. His choice fell on a monk well known to the imperial family and "all the clergy," who "had a great reputation as a grammarian, was not unversed in rhetoric and had an unrivalled knowledge of dogma." Anna goes on:

> The emperor sent for him and commanded him to compile a list of heresies, covering each separately

and appending in each case the refutation, using the texts of the holy fathers. (*Alexiad*, XV.9, trans. Sewter, rev. Frankopan, 459).

Again according to Anna, it was Alexius who named the work the *Dogmatic Panoply*. It was meant as a show-piece, copied in splendid illustrated manuscripts sent out for example to Alexius's new monastery on Patmos, and preceded by a prose preface in praise of Alexius as well as a number of sets of iambic verses.[18] Under Alexius's grandson Manuel I this work was followed, as we have seen, by a similar compilation, the *Sacred Arsenal*, or "holy armoury," also an imperial commission, and headed by verses by George Skylitzes. Dialogue and argument are integral to both these works. In his own *Dogmatic Panoply*, written in Nicaea after the capture of Constantinople in 1204, the historian Niketas Choniates incorporates the dialogue of Soterichos Panteugenos on the sacrifice of Christ mentioned in chapter one above.[19] The first part of the *Sacred Arsenal* contains a dialogue (*dialexis*) between the Emperor Manuel and a group of Roman cardinals on the subjects of Roman primacy and the *Filioque*,[20] while in the second part, which also deals with a range of other heresies from the Byzantine point of view, Armenian representatives also engage in dialogue with Manuel. The argument is supported in both parts by *florilegia*, collections of citations, and by lists of syllogisms. At the end of the first dialogue the cardinals deliver fulsome compliments to the emperor on his skill at debating, allegedly surpassing that of the best dialecticians they had known,[21] just as the fictional Jews in *Adversus Iudaeos* dialogues declare themselves persuaded, or even convert.

These works take as firm a stand against internal wrong belief as they do against "Latin errors," and they also set out uncompromising statements of what they see as orthodoxy. Whether either these or the other anti-Latin works should be taken at face value is quite a different matter. Clearly we can agree that the anti-Latin works were also a way of expressing internal needs and internal insecurities,[22] but they also need to be placed in a denser context of textual production. As for the compendia, while the first was commissioned from a monastic writer, the second and third were the work of a high official connected with the imperial family, and a major historian and office-holder respectively;[23] they cannot be written off as if they had only marginal importance. It is telling that in his *History* Niketas Choniates is critical of Manuel I's religious interventions, and shows sympathy with persons who were condemned on doctrinal grounds, but that the *Panoply*, with a different purpose, takes a different line.[24]

70

These and other underlying tensions and dynamics need to be explored further.

In practice these works have mostly been ignored or put aside in mainstream scholarship, and Niketas's *Panoply* is often dismissively described as a reworking of that of Zigabenus (to which it was certainly much indebted). But Niketas's *Panoply* was not the result of an imperial commission, and describes itself as having been sent to an anonymous friend, so it is at least reasonable to think that it expresses the author's own intentions. According to Luciano Bossina, Niketas composed it after 1204 as a defence of orthodoxy in the face of the appointment of a Latin patriarch in Constantinople, although Niccolò Zorzi argues for its having been written over a longer period, at least in part while Niketas was still in Constantinople.[25] These works are the indispensible complement and toolbox for the actual discussions that had been going on with the Latins, not to mention the Armenians in the case of the *Sacred Arsenal*, and they also provided arguments against Jews and Muslims. They were read and used, as can be seen not only from their manuscript history but also from citations, and from the use made of them by later writers, whether in the form of adaptation and appropriation, or, as sometimes, refutation. In the early thirteenth century John Bekkos wrote a careful refutation of Kamateros's comments on the patristic texts cited in the *Sacred Arsenal*, while at the same time acknowledging Kamateros's skill and standing; and many others, including Nicephorus Blemmydes and Nicholas Mesarites, drew heavily on the work or regarded it as an authority. We may well ask from our modern perspective why such compilations were produced, or even more pertinently, why they went on being produced. But their reception history shows how seriously they were taken and how centrally important they were; as their titles suggest, they provided essential tools for use in the context of the deep divisions that remained in place not merely for decades but over several centuries.

Yet while they purport to assert and demonstrate orthodoxy through the condemnation of wrong belief, these texts are in themselves indicative of profound internal disagreements. Twelfth-century Byzantium was not one-track in its doctrinal views, and contemporaries disagreed passionately on many issues, from matters such as the propriety of melting down church treasures and the interpretation of Gospel passages to their attitudes towards the Latins. We would not have these works if that were not so.

The notion of competition also applies. Like many contemporary theological dialogues, the compendia are about proof; accordingly *florilegia*, collections of citations appended to prove points in the argument, were a central feature.[26] Proofs could also take the form of lists of syllogisms. According to Hans-Georg Beck, the works of the twelfth-century Eustratius of Nicaea marked the "triumph" of syllogistic in Byzantine theology.[27] Eustratius appended a "demonstration through syllogisms" to his dialogue about icons, and the first part of the *Sacred Arsenal* contains a list of 42 syllogisms and 151 citations, the total for the whole work amounting according to Bucossi to some 210 syllogisms and 1300 proof texts.[28]

The practice of amassing lists of citations had been in place for centuries, certainly since the doctrinal disputes of the fifth century in connection with the Councils of Ephesus and Chalcedon, and had been honed in many controversies subsequently, especially during the period of iconoclasm and at the major church councils.[29] That did not mean that the lists of citations were taken on board ready made—rather, the choice depended on the argument in hand. We must think in terms of a vast body of floating material available to be utilized in different ways for different purposes. The ability to amass and deploy patristic citations was a key part of the essential repertoire of anyone who engaged in these discussions.

As for syllogisms, the emperor is praised in the dedicatory verses to the *Sacred Arsenal* for his unanswerable syllogisms on the subject of the *Filioque* and for the Scriptural syllogisms he deployed against the Armenians. Manuel also argued by means of syllogisms in his two-day debate with the patriarch Nicholas Mouzalon, this time in favour of the view that the latter should step down because of irregularities in his election; again he did so even while accusing his dialogical opponent Mouzalon of sophistry.[30] A good deal of posturing went on: despite their own liking for syllogisms, the Byzantines professed to be suspicious of syllogistic, and frequently expressed disapproval of dialectic, even in the very texts that depended on both.[31] It would be rash therefore to say that the Byzantine theological debates are where philosophical training, rhetoric and theology met, if that implies some kind of resolution; on the contrary, they indicate a deep uncertainty and perhaps disquiet. They also show the enormous importance that was attached to debate.

Latins and Greeks meet and talk

The *Dogmatic Panoply* of Zigabenus belongs to Alexius's programme for the assertion of orthodoxy in the early part of our period. The *Sacred Arsenal* on the other hand was commissioned in the early 1170's, in the years following Manuel I's Edict of 1166, when he had forced through his own doctrinal position on the Gospel text "The Father is greater than I" with a great fanfare and a display text in Hagia Sophia, and when he was also engaging in discussions with the Armenians. The relevant synodal decree praises Manuel for himself drawing up the list of patristic citations as well as formulating the theological argument. This then is the broader twelfth-century context for the public debates with western representatives that took place over the period, notably in 1112 with Peter Grossolano, the archbishop of Milan, and later with Anselm of Havelberg, who paid visits to Constantinople and Thessalonike in the 1130s and 1150s.

In connection with the visit of Peter Grossolano of Milan while en route for Jerusalem, the patriarch John VIII of Jerusalem had composed a dialogue, perhaps in Constantinople, though the dramatic setting of the dialogue is Jerusalem, between himself and a "Latin philosopher" on the subject of unleavened bread in the Eucharist ("azymes"). It starts with a literary introduction and an exchange about the rules of dialogue. There are at least thirteen manuscripts but, as often, no modern edition. Here too the Byzantine author refers to the "sophisms" of the Latin speaker (*sophistikoi logoi*), from which he says he is protected by the "armoury of faith," and an elaborate play is made in which the Latin asks the Byzantine for help in understanding through teaching, which John says requires *apodeixis* (demonstration) and argument (*protaseis*).[32] We can see both a focus on procedure, and a hostility to the Latins, who are portrayed as treacherous and in need of instruction. Also in Constantinople, Niketas "of Maroneia," archbishop of Thessalonike, composed six dialogues between Latins and Greeks on the *Filioque*, showing considerable sympathy towards the Latins. Interestingly, the prologue to the first explains his use of the dialogue form both as being particularly suited to the technical argument about the procession of the Holy Spirit, and also because of the many precedents. According to Niketas, its goal should be the resolution of differences. He also makes it clear that the personages, a Greek and a Latin, are fictional.[33]

Niketas was one of the Byzantines whose sympathies inclined them towards the Latin position. He has been likened to the Italian Hugo Eteriano, a voluminous pro-Latin author and protégé of Manuel I,[34] a Pisan layman who had studied Aristotle in Paris and was living in Constantinople. Hugo was a supporter of Pope Alexander III. He was also one of several Latins close to the emperor, took part in theological debates in Constantinople and was commissioned by Manuel to explain the Latin position, drawing on citations from Augustine. Hugo was also well aware of the need for Greek patristic texts to be translated into Latin. He debated with the Byzantine Nicholas of Methone, and, as he explains in a letter, was later commissioned by the emperor to take part in discussion of the Latin position in the synod of 1166. A detailed account survives of Hugo's activities, composed by his brother Leo; in it Hugo is described as engaging in "forceful disputation." Leo also describes his brother's various services to the emperor.[35] Hugo also wrote on Greek doctrinal errors, apparently originally in Greek, as he could write in both languages (he was "perfectly learned in both the Greek and Latin languages," as he was described by the Pisan delegation in 1168 which asked him for advice on heretics in Italy; he answered with reference to Greek patristic authorities).[36] The emperor requested from Hugo a work in three books explaining the Latin position on the Holy Spirit and the Trinity on the basis of Greek authorities and using syllogistic reasoning.[37] It started from earlier discussions by Manuel with eminent Latin cardinals, and Hugo refers in it to his own debates. Hugo's brother Leo was himself employed by the Emperor Manuel as an interpreter at the Byzantine court. Translation was an important activity in these and other matters and when the first debate of Anselm of Havelberg against Niketas of Nicomedia took place in 1136 in the Pisan merchant quarter of

Constantinople, a team of Italian potential interpreters was on hand.

We have here traces of a half-hidden world of constant discussion and debate, some of which became the subject of written dialogues. There must have been more of these than have survived; many of those we do have do not survive in their original form, while relatively few have as yet been properly studied or even edited.

I have perhaps spent too much time on Hugo Eteriano, a Latin, after all; but his case does bring out the complexities against which these discussions and written dialogues took shape. Hugo was an interstitial figure, living in Constantinople, writing in both Latin and Greek, and learned in Greek patristics; he knew not only John of Damascus and John's follower Theodore Abu Qurrah, the ninth-century bishop of Harran, but also the late seventh-century work by Anastasius of Sinai known as the *Hodegos*, and much other material relating to the theological issues about images.[38] His work against the "Patarenes," in Latin, is directed at a Latin community living in Constantinople, whose members Bernard Hamilton identifies with the Cathar followers of the Niketas who conducted a mission to Cathars in the west in 1167. More important for us here, however, is the fact that Hugo's tract shows the extent of contemporary mobility, or what we would now call migration, and the spread of ideas as well as of people, between Constantinople's substantial but also disparate Latin community, and other regions.[39] Tia Kolbaba suggests that the pro-Latin attitude of Manuel I, and an increasing awareness among the Byzantines of the strengths of Latin reasoning, were among the factors that led to the rise in hostility against Latins that culminated in their expulsions in 1182.[40] As for Hugo himself, he managed to flee from Constantinople when the anti-Latin riots broke out and went to Rome, where he was quickly ordained and rose to be a cardinal.

The reports of debates with the Latins, and the related stand-alone dialogue works, co-existed with literary dialogues and with dialogues on other theological issues, such as the religious differences with the Armenians, or the controversy about the Father and the Son that resulted in Manuel's decree of 1166. Imperial policy, diplomatic relations and internal rivalries all played a part in these compositions. There may still be a long way to go in terms of scholarship on these debate and dialogue texts, but it is surely obvious that whatever the religious and other underlying issues they represent, their presentation also links them to the other literary and cultural production of the period.

The *Sacred Arsenal*

I would like to return briefly to the *Sacred Arsenal*, of the early 1170s, for which we are indebted to the work of Alessandra Bucossi, the editor of its anti-Latin part and author of a number of important articles on the text as well as a forthcoming English translation. The *Sacred Arsenal* is a compound work, dealing with arguments against both the Latins and the Armenians. It also exemplifies traits I have already mentioned, in that it has both patristic citations and a collection of syllogisms. Kamateros himself says in his introduction that the emperor (I quote Bucossi's translation) "wanted the quotations from almost every holy book that are useful for the refutation of every single heresy, and indeed those demonstrative syllogisms woven during the dialogues that took place on various occasions by his most inspired mind and tongue, to be written down."[41]

The work illustrates the Byzantine awareness of intellectual developments in the west, though their refutation would need more than appeals to patristic tradition and anti-Latin prejudice. It also incorporates a dialogue between the Emperor Manuel and a group of Latin cardinals. More like question-and-answer than a stand-alone dialogue, Manuel naturally has the longer speeches and is the successful one. But despite

Kamateros's claims, we may well wonder about the actual relation of text to reality. It shows many similarities with the six dialogues on the procession of the Holy Spirit by Niketas "of Maroneia," who according to Bucossi is likely to have been present at various meetings connected with the synod of 1166.[42] However, while Niketas and Kamateros would probably both have attended the actual discussions, and have had access to records taken then, they did not produce identical texts. This suggests that the written versions reflect authorial decisions, and Bucossi explains the difference by the different aims of the two authors: unlike Kamateros, Niketas was not writing to glorify or justify the emperor, and could thus be fairer to both sides.[43]

The world of such dialogues and synodal discussions was one of "competitive exegesis," a useful concept borrowed from Talal Asad, writing of the different context of contemporary Islam, in a discussion concerned precisely with the challenge of "maintaining orthodoxy in conditions of change and contest."[44] Where there are sacred texts and a strong valuation of tradition, the choice and use of citations, and the different ways of recording actual discussions take on extraordinary importance. Symbolism is also important: the official *Synodikon of Orthodoxy*, produced after the ending of iconoclasm in AD 843, and the decree of Manuel I inscribed in red letters in Hagia Sophia in 1166 both clearly had a powerful symbolic impact, and the same applies, I would argue, for the compendia themselves. Yet the statements of orthodoxy such as we find in the *Sacred Arsenal* and related texts, or in the *Synodikon of Orthodoxy*, to which condemnations of John Italus and Eustratius of Nicaea were added, have a significance that is far more than symbolic. Given that Byzantium was a pre-modern society which attempted to maintain strong religious boundaries, these texts and the techniques they use—citation, naming, choice of terminology—represent a sphere within which disagreement is revealed and its control announced; within it, dialogues were especially suited to express the possibilities of disagreement, even if they could produce no more than a rhetorical resolution or closure.

Anselm of Havelberg and his visits to Constantinople and Thessalonike

The dialogue texts between Latins and Greeks from twelfth-century Constantinople belong in the context not only of intense argument but also of similar compositions, though sometimes with different agendas, in the west. Discussion about the differences between

Latins and Greeks was a current topic in the west as well as in Byzantium, for instance at the Council of Bari in 1098. No debate text survives from those discussions, but Anselm of Canterbury summarized his own arguments made there against the Greeks in his treatise *On the Procession of the Holy Spirit*. As his biographer tells us, he was persuaded by the pope to take on the task at Bari of refuting the Greeks in a "rational and catholic disputation."[45]

There was already a deep context for Latin-Greek argument on the subject. Let us turn now to a very well-known western visitor to Byzantium in the twelfth century, about whom a great deal has already been written. This is the Anselm of Havelberg already mentioned, the follower of the reformer Norbert of Xanten, who debated with Niketas of Nicomedia during the reign of the Emperor John II Comnenus in Constantinople in 1136 while on a mission on behalf of the Emperor Lothar. He was sent to the east again by the pope in the 1150s, when Pope Hadrian IV and the Emperor Manuel had common interests against the Normans, and talk was briefly of union (the alliance fell apart and any prospects of union with it); on this occasion Manuel sent him to Thessalonike to debate with its metropolitan, Basil Achridenos.

The records of the first debate, or rather, a version by one of the participants, survive in Latin, in fact written by Anselm himself well over a decade later, seemingly at the behest of Pope Eugenius III, with the key topics as azymes, Roman primacy and the *Filioque*.[46] Anselm tells us in his prologue that in the year before the time of writing he had been present at Eugenius's court and that the pope had told him of the recent visit of a bishop sent as an envoy by the Emperor Alexius and his unacceptable arguments about the *Filioque* and azymes. Anselm told the pope that he had himself been an envoy in Constantinople, where he had stayed "for a long time, conducting many conversations and debates of this nature, sometimes private and sometimes public, about the doctrine and ritual respectively maintained by Latins and Greeks."[47]

The pope then directed him to "gather into one work what I had said in Constantinople and what I heard or understood others to say—that I write down a sort of *Anticeimenon*, that is a book of controversies, in dialogue form." Anselm thus makes no pretence of recording a single debate or set of debates (and indeed the first book is not a dialogue at all), but he does say that as far as he could remember it, he has "maintained the tone of the dialogue I held with the learned and venerable archbishop of Nicomedia, Niketas, at a public meeting in the city of Constantinople." To this report he added "certain additions as essential for the faith and appropriate for this work." According to

Anselm, Niketas was learned and eloquent, and was the leader of twelve teachers, *didaskaloi*, who ruled on matters of faith and doctrine,[48] a claim sitting well with Anselm's natural aim of impressing his audience with his own skill in facing such an opponent.

The tone of the so-called *Anticeimenon* which resulted, and which at least in part purports to convey a debate held in Constantinople with Niketas, is irenic, and directed at a western audience. It is also clearly pedagogic, with several references to the ways in which Anselm is making a difficult argument accessible.[49] Anselm admits that he does not represent Niketas's actual words, and indeed defends himself for not giving a literal translation. In fact the three books are written from the western perspective, and clearly serve other purposes besides, or instead of, that of recording a debate; their English translators refer to them as "a primer" on the issues covered. The extensive secondary literature on the text is also largely written by western medievalists, for whom Anselm is regarded as an important figure in the reform movement.[50] His supposed ecumenical aims are also stressed; Niketas's unlikely proposal in the work for a universal council is described by one scholar as a "gracious escape from the impasse of debate." According to the same modern author, book 1 is "a statement of the dilemma between hierarchic obedience and charity," and an "apology for peace and Christian charity among clerical factions," expressing a view of religion on Anselm's part "as an unfolding dilemma of a critic at prayer."[51] For another western medieval scholar, Anselm offers "one of the most thorough discussions of the papacy at this time."[52]

A closer look is obviously needed from the Byzantine point of view. In the work Niketas admits that primacy of honour to Rome had been agreed by the Emperor Phocas—that is, that it had been granted by an emperor. We might well doubt whether this is what Niketas actually said, or whether he also agreed that their differences were slight, or that he could have proposed an ecumenical council himself (an imperial prerogative), especially as this is purportedly followed in the dialogue by enthusiastic acclamations of approval. What we have here is a Latin construct addressing Latin issues and audiences (Anselm's "brothers," seemingly members of Norbert's Praemonstratensian order). It is designed to reassure them of Anselm's success as much as to record the actual arguments of both sides.

The work is complex. The first book is an essay on the history of the church with a focus on the rise of western monasticism and Anselm's own order, in which he responds to his critics. As for books 2 and 3, which do claim to record the dialogue, the prologue to book 2, on the *Filioque*, tells us that it took place in the Pisan quarter in Constantinople, near to the church of St Irene, with silentiaries and notaries present, and many Latins, including Moses, an Italian from Bergamo, who is chosen as the interpreter. One of the three Italians named, from among whom Moses was selected, is James of Venice, himself the translator into Latin of Aristotle's *Topics* and *Sophistical Refutations*. We see clearly here the key importance of translations, and this is where Niketas asks for a literal translation, which Anselm refuses. Book 3 has more to say on the occasion and the audience, and the conclusion is met with acclamations in both Greek and Latin. In the view of Jay Lees,[53] Anselm is writing for his partisans, and his readers are his wider audience, who are also in a sense witnesses to the dialogue. Lees sees the dialogue as essentially a piece of theatre, "a theatrical presentation of the unity of the faithful," and "an image of performed action in which Anselm invites his readers to participate as members of the audience." Indeed Anselm himself uses theatrical language ("theatrical representations," *similitudines scaenicae*) to describe the beneficial effects of disputation in conveying instruction.[54] For Lees, the dialogue conveys shifting positions, "a moving picture," yet one that has to seem to be real in order to convince Anselm's readers; thus its theatricality is essential to the persuasive function of the dialogue.[55] He goes on, "Nicetas is a literary construct, however much he may be based on a real man" yet he is "neither a straw man nor a buffoon, but a sympathetic man of faith."[56] Nevertheless the Niketas of the dialogue remains the construction of Anselm. I wonder if the real Niketas ever read, or had translated for him, what Anselm had come up with.

Much less has been written about the second occasion on which Anselm debated with a Byzantine. In the first case we can see that he had several agendas of his own in addition to the main items of religious difference between Greeks and Latins. This time Anselm was sent directly by Pope Hadrian IV, in the context of the latter's wish to forge alliances abroad, and his interlocutor, Basil, the metropolitan of Thessalonike, also corresponded with Hadrian IV after the meeting, praising him as a pastor, which is how the Byzantines liked to see the popes.[57] The Emperor Manuel received Anselm in Constantinople but then sent him to debate with Basil in a debate that lasted over two days and which emphasized the role of secular *paideia* as a necessary preparation for theology. Basil was well connected, and a member of the social network of the scholar John Tzetzes, who addressed two learned letters to him; he had read Tzetzes's commentary on the difficult Alexandrian poet Lycophron.[58] He was also the author of a funerary oration for the Emperor Manuel's first wife Eirene (Bertha of Sulzbach), who died in 1159, and was clearly chosen on that occasion for his learning and skill. The tone on both sides in the dialogue is notably conciliatory. But though it was known for instance to Basil's successor Eustathius of Thessalonike, the dialogue has been little studied by modern scholars, and the edition of 1901 is based on only four of the known manuscripts.[59] Magdalino includes it in a list of debates and dialogues that he says "purport to be exact transcriptions,"[60] and in the context already mentioned of dismissive remarks about "potted arguments." He sees it as part of a "growing mood of entrenchment against doctrinal outsiders." But as we have seen, and as Tia Kolbaba has argued, there is more complexity and more variation in this literature than this suggests.

Heresy-hunting in Byzantium?

Given what was happening in the west in this period, and since I have largely used the term without comment, a little more needs to be said about heresy in the Byzantine context. It must be stressed that we know very little about any "popular" movements in twelfth-century Byzantium, or reform movements coming from below; the dualist Bogomils who were one of Alexius's targets remain shadowy and hard to identify with precision, even if they found some elite sympathisers.[61] In Byzantine terms the term "heresy" was applied much more widely, to designate any and every kind of wrong belief, however intellectual, and of course "wrong," in the judgement of whichever group or individual was doing the labelling. Contemporaries who held heterodox doctrinal views were commonly classed together with, and referred to as, long-ago "heretics" such as Arians, Messalians or Novatians—as well as being put in the same category as Jews and Muslims. This is a labelling technique, not a serious description,[62] and I will return to it in the next chapter. Classification and labelling of this sort had been built into the vast number of heresiological treatises composed since early Christian times, and were still fundamental ("Hellene," when applied to non-Christians, is just such a label). In our period Latins were incorporated into the same framework. All this makes judging what was really going on extremely hard, and needs to be constantly borne in mind when approaching the debate texts between Latins and Greeks.[63] The logic of this construction of "heresy" in multiple forms is just that: construction. The Byzantines constructed "Latin" errors just as much as the Latins suspected Byzantium.[64] Even the categories "east" and "west," so familiar to us, are as slippery as those of "heretic" or "orthodox."[65] The Latin-Greek dialogues are a perfect example of such construction and identity-assertion.

Peter Grossolano

Thus if we go backwards in time to consider the debates on the *Filioque* and Roman primacy earlier in the century, in which Peter Grossolano of Milan took part in Constantinople in 1112, it makes a difference that we must rely partly on a description made by the very same Eustratius of Nicaea with whom I began in chapter one. He may or may not have taken part himself; either way, he makes no pretence of sticking to what was actually said during the three-day talks. Not surprisingly, his description is written very much from the Byzantine point of view and in support of the Greek position, thus exactly the opposite of what we saw in the case of Anselm of Havelberg. Unlike that of Anselm, his tone is hostile, with the Latins often represented as arrogant and bold.[66] Grossolano had written his own pamphlet,[67] which was read out in front of the Emperor Alexius, and Eustratius's aim was to provide further arguments against the new points introduced by Grossolano, while also taking the opportunity to showcase Alexius's debating skills (he says the emperor produced "cartloads of arguments"). The actual debate took place in the presence of the emperor and of a gathering that may refer to the Synod, and John Phournes has also left his own version (of which yet again there is no critical edition).[68] Others who took part were Theodore of Smyrna, encountered in the *Timarion* discussed in chapter one, and Niketas Seides, who was later to turn against Eustratius.[69] Again there is no critical edition of Eustratius's account, and some speeches also made after the debate remain unpublished. However there are several manuscripts of Eustratius's text, indicating that the work found readers. The argument was in fact critical, for although nothing came of it, Alexius was toying with the idea of union, and wanted to exert influence in the west. If anything, this means that the actual arguments were even more of a construction designed to represent the Latins as opponents.

Greeks, Latins and Hellenes

In debates like these we often find the speakers designated respectively as the Latin and the Greek (*Graikos*). The term "Hellene" had for centuries been appropriated to refer disparagingly to pagans, and was still so used, for instance of John Italus under Alexius I Comnenus. In this usage "Hellenes" were suspect, likely to be dangerous Platonists, and therefore heretics. But after centuries in which the Byzantines identified themselves as "Romans," they finally began by the mid-twelfth century to allow themselves to be identified as Hellenes, not in proto-nationalist terms, but to differentiate themselves from the Romans of Old Rome (as opposed to Constantinople, the New Rome) and by way of expressing a cultural memory of classical Greece, even a "nostalgia" for classical Athens.[70]

The meaning of Hellenism in a wider sense is one of the most difficult and controversial issues in Byzantine studies. The word itself can mean many different things, and in the case of Byzantium it is often discussed by modern scholars in terms of literary production.[71] Thus Stratis Papaioannou refers to Hellenism as a "sociolect for the educated elite" in the eleventh century, and to "literary Hellenism" as "a learned man's sociolect."[72] Hellenism could also be a mask for an author, and adopting a classicizing manner was certainly the pathway to literary success. But the term Hellenism also suggests an ethnic meaning, and is also inextricably connected in modern discussions with ideas of national identity in modern Greece, a narrative in which the place of Byzantium is claimed by some and hotly denied by others. One does not need to accept the nation-state argument of Anthony Kaldellis or the essentialist one of Niketas Siniossoglou in relation to the continuity of Hellenism in Byzantium to see that use of the term Hellenes is also a matter of a broader contemporary identity politics,[73] an identity politics that we have seen in the Latin and Greek doctrinal debates, and that we will also see in the works written about Jews and Muslims. Twelfth-century Byzantines sometimes called themselves Hellenes for cultural, not for ethnic or proto-nationalist reasons.

So were these dialogues in some sense about Byzantine identity? Any such suggestion must be approached with great caution, given the vast amount of publication on "identity." Particular problems also abound in any attempt to assert a single Byzantine identity, given the existence at all times of multiple identities and ways of self-representation.[74] The extent to which Byzantine or East Roman identity or identities need to be understood in a wider context than that of imperial Constantinople is also a lively current question. Even within the terms of a focus on Constantinople scholars have also projected onto Byzantium their own ideas of what this identity might have entailed. Paul Magdalino wrote in 1992 in terms of Byzantine insecurity and powerlessness, and, as the century wore on, of the sense that New Rome had passed its peak; "the professionally literate of Church and State used their collective memory to boost their collective morale."[75] This now seems like an over-simplification, deriving from an acute modern awareness of the coming disaster of 1204. In general, subjective value judgements and appeals to insecurity fail to do justice to modes of discourse and identity techniques in writing and argument that had their roots centuries before. A broader approach using discourse analysis and drawing on the dialogues that are the subject of this book will produce a more nuanced understanding of the actual levels of complexity both within the "Orthodox establishment" that was supposedly in control and more widely.

Byzantines and Armenians

To conclude this chapter I would like to turn aside briefly to consider the parallel case of debates with the Armenians. As we have seen already, the *Sacred Arsenal* of Kamateros, from the early 1170s, contained dialogues not only with the Latins but also with the Armenians, and considerable effort was put in to bring the latter to conform to Byzantine ideas of orthodoxy. So high on the agenda was the overall diplomatic effort that in 1172 there were embassies in Constantinople from Germany, Rome, Sicily and the

Armenians. If the surviving dialogue is genuine, the emperor demonstrated his zeal by engaging in debate himself with the patriarch Michael III Anchialos.[76] His initiatives towards the Armenians were part of a wider effort to reinforce the influence of Byzantium in the east, which also involved relations with the Syrian Orthodox, and extended to marriage alliances as well as religious diplomacy.[77] The issue was not new. Eustratius of Nicaea had written a discourse against the Armenians in 1114,[78] and the present round of discussions took place over more than a decade, from 1165 to 1179, with the best-known episode concerning the two missions in 1170 and 1172 to the Armenian patriarch at the fortress of Hromkla (today, Rumkale in eastern Turkey) on the Euphrates, west of Edessa, of an official envoy, a certain Theorianos, from whom we have two lengthy *dialexeis* in Greek.[79] This Theorianos was not an ecclesiastic, being described as a *maistor*, a *philosophos* and a "liege-man" of the emperor.[80] For his sympathy towards the Latins Magdalino has connected him with Hugo Eteriano and further suggested that he was a Greek from south Italy. Linda Safran argues that he was from Oria in the Salento, where Greek survived and religious relations were complex. Theorianos himself accepted the Latin custom of using azymes, and points to a letter in which he urged his addresses to "love the Latins as colleagues, for they are Orthodox and children of the Catholic and Apostolic church, just like yourselves."[81] Theorianos was well able to conduct technical debates on the issues dividing the orthodox Byzantines and the miaphysite Armenians. These had been preceded by other discussions, including one in Constantinople with the emperor, and through the medium of official letters,[82] though not surprisingly Manuel rejected the invitation to travel himself to debate with the Armenians at Hromkla. An Armenian chronicler wrote of the many books that Theorianos loaded onto a mule for his arduous journey east,[83] and the two accounts of his meetings reveal discussions that lasted over some days, punctuated by interruptions and meetings of the Armenian synod. Theorianos takes the initiative, delivers long speeches—though the Armenian *katholikos* Nerses IV Šnorhali ("the Gracious") also speaks "all day"—and cites Greek and some Latin patristic texts. The first dialogue also introduces a Syrian bishop, John of K'esun, whose attempts to persuade the *katholikos* not to yield are reported to Theorianos by a teacher (*didaskalos*) called Vartan, who is said not to speak properly, that is, by using syllogisms and appeals to authority, but "contentiously"[84]—in other words, like the Latins as perceived by the Byzantines. On the next day the Syrian joins the discussion between Theorianos and Nerses but does not speak, claiming that it is wrong to intervene in discussions not his own. Stephen, another *didaskalos*, then takes up the exchange with Theorianos.

These dialogues are well known,[85] although yet again there is still no critical edition. They read like the reports of fairly protracted talks, are cast in direct speech, and contain hints of the real situation: for instance Theorianos does not know Syriac, but offers Nerses a document in Syriac to read, which Nerses has to have translated. The level of acquaintance with Greek on the part of the Chalcedonian Armenian who was Theorianos's partner is an issue raised in the first dialogue, and we also learn that an official interpreter called Michael carried the emperor's letter to Nerses.[86] There are also official and unofficial copies of the letters between Nerses and Manuel.[87] Theorianos claims to have succeeded in his mission, but the Armenians presented it otherwise to themselves, as is clear from a hagiographic *Life* of Nerses, which glosses over Nerses's submission and claims that Theorianos recounted his holiness and sanctity in Constantinople in such glowing terms to the ecclesiastics and members of the imperial family in the palace that everyone rejoiced and all traces of hostility to Armenians disappeared.[88] According to Christopher MacEvitt, Nerses's apparent accommodation towards the Byzantines was in fact a show for domestic consumption, aimed at the

Armenian *vardapets*.[89] Both the Armenian and the Byzantine sides claimed success from their very different perspectives, and dialogues with the Armenians were replayed shortly afterwards in the *Sacred Arsenal*. But with the deaths of Nerses in 1173 and Manuel in 1180 whatever union had been achieved, if any, was abandoned, and in 1193 the Armenians made an alliance with the Latins. Such was the reality of this inter-confessional diplomacy. The two dialogues of Theorianos provide a rare example where a dialogue, or dialogues, can be set alongside plentiful other material.

In my last chapter I will be looking at Byzantine writings about Jews and Muslims in the long twelfth century, comparing and contrasting them with western writing about and attitudes to Jews in the same period, and arguing that these too need to be integrated into any general discussions of Byzantine culture and society. As for the anti-Latin works, they have as yet been largely discussed only in partial and strictly theological terms, and without a real overview or taking into account the serious lack of critical editions. Nor are all of them straightforwardly classifiable as "polemic." My argument has been that these works have more to tell us, and not only for the twelfth century, if we try to bring them into an integrated picture of intellectual and literary production.

99

Chapter 3

Jews and Muslims

In this final chapter I want to connect with what I have discussed up to now a body of literature that seems at first sight both recalcitrant and limited. I refer to the Byzantine dialogues with, or against, Jews and Muslims (often termed polemics in modern scholarship without further discussion). Latin dialogues between Christians and Jews, known as *Adversus Iudaeos* texts, were regularly produced in the west in the long twelfth century, and Greek and Syriac examples had also had a long history already in Byzantium. They were joined as time went on by a parallel strand of dialogues and other works directed against Islam. Can dialogues of this kind be linked with the others we have discussed so far? And surely they must relate to the actual conditions of Byzantine-Jewish and Byzantine-Muslim relations in this turbulent period?

At the end of the thirteenth century the Florentine Dominican Riccoldo da Monte Croce spent several years in Baghdad, learned Arabic and wrote about his travels, trying to understand how Islam fitted into the divine plan.[1] The writings on Jews and Muslims in twelfth-century Constantinople that are my subject are very different from his, as also from the wonderfully rich material Natalie Davis was able to exploit for the sixteenth century in *Trickster Travels*.[2] Moreover, like several other western contemporaries, Riccoldo's approach to Islam derived from a firm position of Christian superiority.[3] Nevertheless, I will argue that, like the anti-Latin treatises and dialogues, Byzantine dialogues against Jews and Muslims should also be read in a broad contemporary context; in addition they should be brought together with the high-style literary texts to help us understand the cognitive, and therefore the social, world of the day.

Byzantines and Jews

The Jewish population of Constantinople, Thessalonike and Thebes was described in the 1160s by the well-known Jewish traveller Benjamin of Tudela,[4] and according to him comprised more than two thousand in the capital, with other communities elsewhere in the empire. In Constantinople Jews were divided into Rabbanites and Karaites, and included learned Hebrew scholars.[5] Evidence from the Cairo Genizah suggests that there were Jewish schools in Thebes and Thessalonike, and that Jews were not just traders and merchants, especially in the silk and tanning industries, but also included scholars engaged in Biblical exegesis and the study of the Mishnah and Talmud.[6] Benjamin is one of the best-known sources on Jews in the period, and wrote of the Jews he met in Spain, southern France, Italy, the Holy Land, Baghdad and Persia. He was impressed by Constantinople but thought the condition of Jews there was bad. It is worth quoting the passage:

> No Jews live in the city, for they have been placed behind an inlet of the sea. An arm of the sea of Marmora shuts them in on the one side, and they are unable to go out except by way of the sea, when they want to do business with the inhabitants. In the Jewish quarter are about 2,000 Rabbanite Jews and about 500 Karaïtes, and a fence divides them.[7] Amongst the scholars are several wise men, at their head being the chief rabbi R. Abtalion, R. Obadiah, R. Aaron Bechor Shoro, R. Joseph Shir-Guru, and R. Eliakim, the warden. And amongst them there are artificers in silk and many rich merchants. No Jew there is allowed to ride on horseback. The one exception is R. Solomon Hamitsri, who is the king's physician, and through whom the Jews enjoy consid-

erable alleviation of their oppression. For their condition is very low, and there is much hatred against them, which is fostered by the tanners, who throw out their dirty water in the streets before the doors of the Jewish houses and defile the Jews' quarter. So the Greeks hate the Jews, good and bad alike, and subject them to great oppression, and beat them in the streets, and in every way treat them with rigour. Yet the Jews are rich and good, kindly and charitable, and bear their lot with cheerfulness. The district inhabited by the Jews is called Pera. (trans. Adler)

Despite the information provided by Benjamin, the history of Jews and Judaism in Byzantium is much harder to grasp than that of Jews in the medieval west. As Nicholas de Lange points out, the fact that there is far less evidence from Byzantium has been an impediment to general historians and specialists alike.[8] Moreover, as with the scholarship on some of the key debates on the *Filioque*, the standard focus in studies of medieval Christian-Jewish relations is on the west. This is still the case in the fundamental history of Jewish-Christian controversy originated by Samuel Krauss and revised and edited by William Horbury, where a rich discussion of the eleventh and twelfth-century west contrasts with just a few pages of summary on Byzantium.[9] Yet while the route by which the Hebrew language arrived in Europe is still unclear, and Hebrew scholarship in Byzantium has not been fully studied, the work of Nicholas de Lange in particular suggests that it was more active and more extensive than has usually been imagined.

Byzantium had inherited a tradition of writing about Jews and Judaism that went back to the early Christian period and was based on Hellenistic Judaism. In contrast, in the twelfth-century west, the Jewish convert Peter Alfonsi initiated the critique of the Talmud by Christian writers, in which he was followed by Peter the Venerable, who claimed that the Talmud had reduced the Jews to a subhuman level. Much of the argument in Byzantine Christian literary debates still turned on an exegesis of the Scriptures which had been practised since early Christian times. However, well before the twelfth century, Jews in the Byzantine empire were using Hebrew themselves and producing written works in Hebrew. This changed the situation, though many questions remain, including the difficult issue of which versions of the Bible were used in debates, and what Christians knew of the Hebrew Bible.[10] While we know less about Jews in Byzantium than in the medieval west, this situation is changing, not least thanks to the utilization of material from the Cairo Genizah by de Lange and others.[11] The question of language is also important in considering the extent of actual Jewish-Christian discussion. The documents in the Cairo Genizah include Biblical texts translated into Greek but written in Hebrew script, a Hebrew commentary on Ezekiel in Hebrew with many Greek words, and Hebrew texts with Greek glosses.[12] Knowledge of Greek on the part of Byzantine Jews would have been essential in order for them to engage in discussion with Christians, if indeed they did, and there is evidence for the continued use of Greek, even if written in Hebrew letters, though this is not the same as the sophisticated use of Greek argument needed for theological debate with Christians.

A series of measures are recorded against Jews by Byzantine emperors from Heraclius in the seventh century to Leo III in the eighth and Basil I in the ninth—moves towards forced conversion and/or expulsion.[13] The reasons behind these imperial moves were complex, and none of them remained in force for long or resulted in wholesale conversion;[14] despite claims made for many conversions as a result of Basil I's decree, it was withdrawn by his son and successor Leo VI. In fact Jews had an ambiguous role in Byzantine thinking. Did Christian eschatology require the conversion of the Jews, or were they necessary for Christian salvation? Basil I's efforts met resistance from the ecclesiastical hierarchy and the metropolitan of Nicaea wrote a treatise objecting to the proposed process, arguing that it was not yet time for the "remnant of Israel" to be converted and that this was a matter for the clergy, not for laymen to decide.[15]

Jews held a special position for Christians in another way too. They were "a dialogical necessity;"[16] that is, Christians needed to refute the objections of the Jews in order to assert the truth of Christianity. Argument was the essential tool in this intellectual and religious struggle. The defeat of the Jews, real or not, who featured in such debates was the proof of Christian superiority, and the modes of argument and the range of texts and themes to be debated had been practised and refined in anti-Jewish dialogues and debate texts over many centuries. Anti-Jewish argument had also been ubiquitous in many other Christian texts, not merely dialogues, since early Christian times.[17] The intellectual challenge that Jews still presented to the truth of Christianity explains both the longevity of the *Adversus Iudaeos* literature and its formal aspects. Christian-Jewish conflict is seen in most of our texts as an internal Byzantine religious affair, or even sometimes as a realm of fantasy and wish fulfillment, unlike the indications of real Arab-Byzantine relations that feature for instance in the hagiography of south Italy in the ninth and tenth centuries.[18]

In the eleventh and early twelfth centuries Jews were under attack in various towns in western Europe, both before and after the massacres in the Rhineland in 1096, and works such as those by Peter the Venerable and others in the twelfth century were expressed in a language that would be thought shocking if voiced today.[19] But as we saw, the Jews of Constantinople were well established in the Pera district across the Golden Horn, having been moved there by the authorities, probably in or soon after 1044, when riots in the city were blamed on "many aliens, Armenians, Arabs (i.e., Muslims) and Jews."[20] There was a Jewish cemetery, and matters of jurisdiction for the community were decided by the Byzantine authorities. The Jews had previously lived across the water in the main part of the city, bordering on the areas in the lower part of the Golden Horn populated by Amalfitans and Venetians; the Pisan quarter, where Anselm of Havelberg's first debate took place in 1136, was near St Irene.[21] The Jewish district in the Pera was burned in the events leading up to the capture of Constantinople in 1204, but there were still Jews in Constantinople when Nicolas of Otranto was there between 1205 and 1207 (see below). Jews from Constantinople were also in touch by letter with Jews in Egypt and other places, and Jews from Rus' also came to Constantinople and Thessalonike. Direct literary evidence of real debates between Byzantines and Jews may be sparse, but Nicolas of Otranto claims that he had taken part in such discussions (below), and Krauss and Horbury point to some traces of such debates having happened, and to hints of disputation in Jewish sources.[22] As far as we are aware, these were not like the great staged confrontations that took place in the thirteenth- and fourteenth-century west in 1240, 1263 and around 1375 in Paris, Barcelona and Ávila. Nevertheless they suggest a background of argument on both the Christian and the Jewish sides. Jewish apologetic and polemical literature against Christianity also had a history of its own, as the counterpart of the Christian-Jewish dialogues, and could take the form of dialogues addressed to the *minim*, or heretics, that is, Christians. The Jewish parallel to our Christian dialogues may be submerged, but Judah Hadassi, the twelfth-century Karaite of Constantinople,[23] was far from being the only contemporary Jew to compile Jewish arguments against Christianity.[24]

The *Adversus Iudaeos* literature

Anti-Jewish literature in Greek began in the second century, with Justin Martyr's *Dialogue with Trypho*, in which a Christian convert (Justin) argued against a Jew (Trypho), and in the intervening centuries a large repertoire of well-established tropes and citations had

109

been developed.[25] The *Adversus Iudaeos* literature also flourished in Syriac, particularly in the centuries before and after the emergence of Islam, and may have been influential in the development of Muslim *kalam*, though exactly how is still a subject of discussion. The same tradition also enabled an equivalent literature to develop in which Christian arguments were marshalled against Muslims, and this too flourished in Syriac in the areas under Muslim rule.[26] These types were closely related in technique and sometimes also in substance to the anti-heretical literature mentioned in the last chapter. There is already an enormous secondary literature. Of the Christian-Muslim dialogues, Robert Hoyland has rightly remarked that less work has been done on the later examples than the earlier ones, and the same is true for the Christian-Jewish texts in Greek. However I will consider now the examples in Greek of both types that come more or less from the period I am discussing; the obvious question arises as to how they relate to the actual circumstances, what function they had, and how they compare with the situation in the west. It is not merely a question of how many such works were composed in the period but also of the general awareness of Christian-Jewish argument. Here Patrick Andrist's recent work on the manuscripts and manuscript collections of anti-Jewish works in Greek offers a new direction of research. He surveys the relevant manuscript collections and concludes of our present period that while the numbers of books produced containing earlier anti-Jewish dialogues were not high, their variety is striking. There was clearly a Byzantine readership for the key texts of this kind from the past,[27] and it is reasonable to ask why this should have been so.

In contrast with the position for Byzantium, anti-Jewish writings in Latin from the long twelfth century are both widespread and well studied;[28] they include works by some of the western writers already mentioned in chapter two. At the end of the eleventh century Gilbert Crispin sent a report ("a little debate") of discussions on the subject, with seven set speeches on either side, to Anselm of Canterbury, saying that it arose from argument he had had in London with a learned Jew, educated in Mainz, who was experienced in such disputation and well versed in the Scriptures.[29] In the same period biblical scholarship and Jewish exegesis also flourished in the west, and while we must exercise caution, at least some of the anti-Jewish works seem to hint at personal knowledge of Jews.[30] Strikingly, in contrast with the case of Byzantium, an immensely rich vein of modern scholarship surrounds the whole issue of Jews and Judaism as well as that of contemporary intellectual developments in the medieval west.

111

Nicolas of Otranto

One area where Jews were well-established was south Italy, where there was still a strong Greek and Byzantine connection even after the fall of Bari in 1071.[31] A key text for us to consider comes from there. Shortly after the capture of Constantinople in 1204 a monk from south Italy, Nektarios (formerly Nicolas) of the monastery of Casole and eventually its abbot, visited Constantinople and acted as interpreter as a member of a mission to Byzantium sent by Pope Innocent III. In about 1220 the same Nektarios, or Nicolas, as he is usually called, wrote a long, and until recently still unpublished, dialogue or *Dialexis,* in Greek against the Jews, known only from one fourteenth-century manuscript, in which he says he had conducted many disputations with Jews in Constantinople, Athens, Thessalonike and Thebes.[32] The debate in the text consists of seven discussions over four days and seems to be set in Otranto in modern Puglia, with its Jewish and Greek population. Otranto was one of the places visited in the 1160s by Benjamin of Tudela, when according to him it had five hundred Jews.[33] Nicolas's work can be read as a view from the perspective of southern Italy and indeed from the Roman side (Nicolas was also a translator of Greek into Latin and was sent to Constantinople as interpreter for Cardinal Benedict, legate of Innocent III, and later to Nicaea as legate of the Emperor Frederick II). Scholars have argued that this is "not a real dialogue," that is, the dialogue did not take place as the text implies.[34] Even so, real experience lay behind it. Nicolas says that he had been present at many disputes in Greek cities and debated often with Jews from many places further afield, the citations in the dialogue are in Greek, and the speakers discuss the Greek translations of the Hebrew Scriptures.[35] Nicolas was an in-between figure, drawing on his Byzantine Greek experience in the context of early thirteenth-century south Italy. He also translated liturgical works from Greek into Latin and composed an anti-Latin work using patristic citations and syllogisms and containing elements of dialogue. Poems and letters between Nicolas and his friend George Bardanes the metropolitan of Corfu also survive.[36] Nicolas knew Hebrew as well as Latin, and he knew something of the exegetical differences between Rabbanites and Karaites in relation to the Hebrew Bible as well as their differences of practice.[37] Karaite Jews in the eleventh and twelfth centuries translated Arabic works into Hebrew, and composed Hebrew works of their own. Rivalries between the two groups ran high. Judah Hadassi attacked Rabbanites as well as Christians in his writings, and in Nicolas's dialogue the Jewish speaker

113

is a Rabbanite who reacts with indignation when the Greek asks if he is a Karaite.[38]

In its eschatology and its expectation of the Messiah Évelyne Patlagean compared Nicolas's dialogue with the contemporary Latin *Adversus Iudaeos* text by Joachim of Fiore, which was written in Calabria, and so is also from south Italy, but which is less well informed about Judaism than that of Nicolas.[39] Nicolas's text, which lacks its final folio but seems to have ended with the baptism of the Jew, is oriented towards Greek Byzantine conditions, and the Jew is not the usual stock figure, but an intellectual well able to engage in dialectic.[40] On the other hand, we have seen that Jews could stand for heretics, and in particular, through their denial of the divinity of Christ, for Arians and Nestorians, and a connection is made here between the Jew's arguments and those of Arians and Nestorians.[41] This is the mirror image of what we have already seen in the assimilation of heretics to Jews in the Greek heresiological compendia and anti-heretical texts, and it also recalls the parallel tendency in Christian texts to refer to Bogomils as Messalians.[42] On one level such elisions were no more than familiar rhetorical slurs, and as we saw, in Byzantine heresiology the terms "Arian," "Messalian" and so on, heresies from the early centuries, are constantly applied to contemporary groups, but these were dangerous assimilations in the anti-heretical atmosphere of the west in the period, and Claudio Schiano suggests that the dialogue may reflect contemporary western anxieties about heresy.[43] It is also worth remembering, as he also points out, that Nicolas's dialectical ability and extensive use of earlier source material does not necessarily imply that the issues debated in the text were not real or that Nicolas was not drawing on his own experience.

Dialogues against the Jews in the west and in Byzantium

The situation between Jews and Christians in the west was also affected by the influence of Moorish Spain. Conversion was a particular issue, and not only in relation to Spain. Peter Alfonsi, a Spaniard, and Herman the Jew were both Jewish converts, or at least present themselves as such. According to his autobiographical account of his conversion and baptism, *Opusculum de conversione sua*, Herman was a Jew from Cologne and eventually became a Praemonstratensian canon; before his conversion, which came about as a result of the prayers of others, he says that he had challenged Rupert of Deutz to a public disputation. Peter, converted in Spain in 1106, lived in England and France and composed his *Dialogues against the Jews* around

1100; they consist of twelve exchanges between Moses, that is, Peter's former self, and Peter, his Christian persona, a form that he explains would make it easy to consult, while the dialogue mode would aid the reader's understanding.[44] It is difficult to judge how much credence to attach to the autobiographical elements in these works,[45] but their themes and the prominence of the conversion motif clearly reflect topics and anxieties that were high on contemporary western agendas. Christian Hebraism, that is, the study of the Hebrew language, the Hebrew Bible and Jewish writings, was also a feature of this period in the west and was practised by scholars such as Herbert of Bosham, the adviser of Thomas Becket. This Hebrew scholarship did not always produce negative outcomes.[46] Many scholars, more focused on the idea of rising hostility to Jews, have played down this trend, and placed emphasis on the shriller *Adversus Iudaeos* texts. But putting too much emphasis on the more polemical texts risks obscuring the actual complexity of Christian responses to Jews in the period, while raising the question of how the *Adversus Iudaeos* dialogues relate to other kinds of writing about Jews. But not all dialogues were written by Christians, as we see from the dialogue written in Arabic by Judah Halevi (d. 1141) between a learned Jew and the king of the Khazars, and containing a discussion about the merits of philoso-

116

phy, Christianity, Islam and Judaism. Here, instead of Jews converting to Christianity, the Khazars convert to Judaism—a memory of their actual adoption of Judaism several centuries before. Judah Halevi was a Spanish physician, a learned Hebrew poet and the author of epistles in rhyming prose, who had moved from Toledo to the Muslim south, and who also journeyed via Egypt to Jerusalem.[47] Peter Abelard's *Collationes*, containing discussion about the rival merits of philosophy, Judaism and Christianity, also belong to the 1140s.[48] Abelard's work was not a conventional *Adversus Iudaeos* text but its argument for reason and rational argument as the way to reach conclusions is posed in terms of the superiority of reason over traditional exegesis and similar themes feature in other Latin dialogues with Jews.[49] Reason and logical argument were not of course unknown in Greek anti-Jewish works.[50] I would argue however that it was just this twelfth-century Latin emphasis on reason that stimulated the Byzantine anxiety about dialectic that we have already met.

In the eleventh and twelfth-century a vigorous Jewish culture existed in the west, even if relations between Christians and Jews were often tense and complex. Views vary as to how and why Christian attitudes to Jews in western Europe hardened in the course of the twelfth century, but despite the obvious questions

117

about possible comparison, the huge amount of secondary literature rarely if ever has anything to say about Byzantium.[51] According to Bowman, the Jews of the Byzantine empire were less affected by the issues pressing on their western co-religionists. This may be why examples of the long established genre of *Adversus Iudaeos* texts in Greek within Byzantium are relatively few in this period, although in contrast Robert Bonfil writes of a renewed impulse towards producing such works in the ninth and tenth centuries.[52] As for Byzantine Jews themselves, while, as we saw, polemic against Christians did exist, in general it may well be the case that in the twelfth century they were more engaged in producing their own Hebrew works than in engaging with Greeks. But a lack of Christian Greek dialogue texts in the traditional *Adversus Iudaeos* manner does not mean that Byzantium was more tolerant of Jews; nor does it imply that other kinds of Greek writing were not still permeated by the anti-Jewish themes that had been a feature of Greek Christian literature for centuries. Within Byzantium, the beginning of the Crusades and pressures from contemporary Muslims were both powerful factors which affected attitudes to Jews.[53] One needs to be cautious.

A large part of the modern scholarship on the *Adversus Iudaeos* literature of all periods is still preoccupied with finding "real" debates and "real" Jews. Important as this is, and as understandable as a methodological aim, it can also distort judgements: the histories of Judaism itself and of Christian-Jewish relations are not the only issues that arise when approaching this material, and a closer look at individual texts will often reveal their actual complexity, if not indeed their degree of fictionality. We have seen already how tricky it can be to assume that the dialogue texts that we have represent anything like true records of debates that actually happened, even when we are sure that such a debate did in fact take place, and the case of the *Adversus Iudaeos* texts is particularly difficult in this regard, given their centuries-long history and well-established motifs and literary techniques. There is indeed far more evidence for discussion and for Jewish intellectual life in the west than there is for Byzantium in our period. But regardless of its final form, Nicolas of Otranto's treatise does belong in the contextual background of discussion and talk in Constantinople and other cities in the Byzantine empire. Christian-Jewish dialogues were not immune from the atmosphere of argument in Byzantine society. Like some of the other dialogues I have mentioned already, Nicolas of Otranto's dialogue lets us see something of the broader interactions between Constantinople and the wider world and the transmission of debate between the capital and other Byzantine cities, and between Byzantium and south Italy. This and others of the works mentioned here also play a major discursive role in forming the intellectual patterns pervading contemporary society.

Christian-Muslim dialogues in Byzantium

Let us turn now to the equivalent Byzantine writings about, or against, Muslims. These have similarities in form and approach with the *Adversus Iudaeos* texts, and indeed passages attacking Islam were sometimes included in works dealing principally with Jews or with heresy, as in the case of Zigabenus's *Dogmatic Panoply* and twelfth-century Latin anti-Jewish works such as that by Peter Alfonsi.[54] In some ways Jews and Muslims were perceived similarly: Peter the Venerable, for instance, slips on several occasions from anti-Jewish to anti-Muslim argument.[55] In addition western medieval views of Islam were heavily coloured by prejudice and justification, as well as by lack of knowledge. Writing in the early twelfth century, Guibert of Nogent commented on the lack of good information or theological refutation of Islam, saying that nothing was known of "this new prophet." It was in answer to this situation that Peter the Venerable, abbot of Cluny

and soon afterwards the author of a polemical treatise *Against the Inveterate Obstinacy of the Jews*, travelled to Spain in 1142 and was active in promoting
the translation of the Qur'ān and other Arabic texts
into Latin. Under his auspices an Englishman, Robert
of Ketton, produced the first Latin translation of the
Qur'ān in 1143.[56] Peter referred to such translation
as a "sacred armoury" (*armarium christianum*), a term
reminiscent of the Byzantine anti-heretical compendia already discussed. His own *Contra sectam Sarra-
cenorum* (*Against the Sect of the Saracens*) begins with
a prologue listing Christian heresies in a manner very
similar to the techniques used by John of Damascus
and other Byzantine writers. However the title of the
translation, *The Law of Muhammad the Pseudoprophet*,
and Peter's own works against the heresy of the Saracens make his motivation clear. In general, the Muslims are regarded as "dreadful adversaries," and Islam
is not seen in Peter's or in other contemporary Latin
works as an independent religion. Rather, it is presented as irrational and deviant from Christianity, while
Muhammad is a false prophet and the Qur'ān a mass
of contradictions.

It is not only the attitude taken in these Latin
works but also the history of modern scholarship on
medieval attitudes to Islam that is deeply coloured by
prejudice and underlying motivations. A large mod-

121

ern bibliography exists on western medieval or "European" (Byzantium rarely gets more than a mention) views of Islam, in which questions of East and West and Orientalism are closely intertwined.[57] If these developments are seen in terms of a construction of Western European Christendom, as some would have it, Byzantium is left in an awkward position. Where Byzantium fits in this model (is it Eastern or European?) and how Byzantine Greek writing against Islam compares with that in the Latin west are questions that are not often asked.[58]

The background of anti-Muslim dialogues

In the eastern Mediterranean and the regions under Islamic rule, dialogues against Islam had begun in the seventh century, and followed patterns not dissimilar from those in the *Adversus Iudaeos* texts.[59] In Greek one thinks first of John of Damascus's account of Islam; this is not a dialogue, and it stands as the last chapter in his compendium on heresies, but the so-called *Dispute between a Saracen and a Christian* was also attributed to him, and dialogues of different kinds feature among his works, providing a rich context to which dialogues about Islam also belonged.[60] John's arguments became standard in later Greek anti-Muslim texts, but most other early examples were in Syriac and come from areas now brought under Muslim rule. As time went on, a substantial corpus also developed in Arabic, while the Greek dialogues by or attributed to Theodore Abu Qurrah, ninth-century bishop of Harran in Mesopotamia and disciple of John of Damascus, addressed the needs of local audiences. It has been noted that the authors of Christian texts dealing with Islam written under Muslim rule in the Near East needed to make their own accommodation with their rulers and were more accommodating in tone than those written in Byzantium itself.[61]

Eleventh and twelfth-century writers could and did draw on earlier models. A key example of Byzantine Christian-Muslim polemical literature in Greek was the late ninth-century refutation of the Qur'ān by the otherwise obscure Niketas of Byzantium, who it seems was using an already existing Greek translation of the Qur'ān.[62] Niketas's text, surviving in only one manuscript, set the refutation of Islam in the context of an exposition of Christian orthodoxy stretching to a quarter of the whole, and it became the basis of many later works, including an anti-Muslim work by the monk Euodius, disciple of Joseph the Hymnographer, in the late ninth century. Possibly from the twelfth century is the dialogue (*dialexis*) of the monk Euthymius with a "Saracen,"[63] and Euthymius Zigabenus's *Dogmatic Panoply* contains a refutation of Islam in chapter 28 which is indebted both to Niketas of Byzantium and to John of Damascus's chapter on Islam.[64] Book 20 of Niketas Choniates's *Dogmatic Panoply* (above) deals with the Agarenes and abjuration formulae. As we have seen already, Zigabenus's and Niketas Choniates's works belong in the category of anti-heresiological compendia, and follow John of Damascus, who treats Islam as a Christian heresy. Anti-Muslim compositions flourished more in the thirteenth century and the late Palaiologan period. In the late fourteenth century, indeed, the Emperor Manuel II, who had spent an enforced period at the court of the Sultan in Ankara, thought it worth covering some 300 pages in the modern edition with arguments against Islam presented in dialogue form.[65]

Byzantines and Muslims

By then Byzantine writers were well aware of contemporary western interest in the Qur'ān, and Manuel II's mentor Demetrius Kydones (the translator of Aquinas) had himself translated the Latin refutation of the Qur'ān by Riccoldo da Monte Croce and had sent his work to Manuel in the 1380s as a useful tool for discussion with pro-Turkish Byzantines in Thessalonike.[66] Similarly, in the twelfth century, Manuel I was mindful of the problems presented by Muslim control of former Byzantine territories, and ensured that bishops were still appointed for sees there.[67] Relations on the ground between Muslim Turks and the Christian population in Asia Minor could be difficult, but conversion to Christianity was also an important factor.[68] Equally, practical accommodation was also sought, and Manuel I's policy alternated between rapprochement and offensive; he first allied himself with the Sultan of Konya and then led a force against him that was advertised as a crusade but which led to defeat at Myriokephalon in Phrygia in 1176.[69] Quite apart from Saladin's spectacular successes in the Holy Land in the 1180s, local conditions were often insecure for Christians in Asia Minor.[70] But there were also many Turks in the Byzantine armies, and the terms of conversion from Islam were a further consideration here. Near the end of his reign, in 1180, and only four years after the battle of Myriokephalon, Manuel proposed a change in the requirements for Muslim converts: only Muhammad himself was to be anathematized, not Muhammad's God.[71] This initiative from the emperor, for which Niketas Choniates's *History* provides the most detailed account, met with stiff opposition from the church hierarchy. Not merely Manuel's critics on this occasion but also western writers on Islam in

125

the thirteenth century, including Riccoldo da Monte Croce, tended to see Islam as irrational and verging on paganism, arguing that even Muslim theologians did not themselves believe in it.[72] Characterizations of Muslim views as pagan and Muslims as "Muhammad-worshippers" were useful ways by which Latin writers justified the Crusades, and similar attitudes lay behind the intense opposition that greeted Manuel's apparent willingness to concede that Allah and the Christian God were one and the same.

As on earlier occasions, the emperor himself produced a treatise on the subject; but as had happened in the case of Jewish conversion under Basil I, he had to back down. Feelings ran very high among the clergy, but although Manuel was already ill he was not deterred and returned with a new version. The emperor summoned the clerics and learned theologians to come and meet him at Scutari where he was staying for his health; in the event he was too ill to meet with them but issued the new formulation through a spokesman, together with threats to call a church council if they did not accept. Eustathius of Thessalonike exploded with indignation and an angry Manuel threatened to make an example of him. Eventually both sides backed down, and the anathema was eventually removed.

Formalized though the nature of anti-Muslim writings in Greek may be, I believe they can nonetheless still tell us something useful about the culture of that period. As with the *Adversus Iudaeos* texts, the genre and the arguments offered by Christians against Islam had been established long before. But when articulated by members of the Constantinopolitan elite they nonetheless reflected current situations and wider concerns. Whatever the relation of these texts to real situations, Jews and Muslims stood side by side as hermeneutic and dialogic components in the efforts of contemporary Byzantines to assert their own orthodoxy.

Conversion: Muslims and others

If we now turn to the abjuration formulae imposed on converts from Islam a deeper context will emerge. Conversion, its circumstances and its regulation, were topical issues in parts of the Byzantine empire, and one such formula preserved in two thirteenth-century manuscripts, but probably going back to the late ninth century, shows knowledge of positions taken in the Qur'ān and the *hadith* as well as the standard motifs of anti-Muslim polemic.[73] Among the subjects of its twenty-two anathemas are the Qur'ānic teachings on Jesus, Muhammad's teaching on marriage and divorce, and the status of the sanctuary at

127

Mecca. The collection in which it appears contains formulae for renouncing a variety of heresies including Manichaeism, as well as for converted Jews and Muslims, according to a pattern set in late antiquity, but evidently in use for contemporary purposes in the twelfth century, when three further sets were added for converted Armenians, Jacobites and Bogomils.[74]

The formulae for Muslim converts, and the collection as a whole, probably date from the ninth century, following the Byzantine-Arab wars, when prisoners were expected to convert. As for Jews, perhaps the most serious hostility came in the tenth century, and possibly in response to external relations.[75] Baptism—also a literary trope—was the holy grail of the Greek *Adversus Iudaeos* texts, so much so that in the possibly tenth-century dialogue of Gregentius and the Jew Herban, the fictive end of the dialogue is imagined as a miracle, with an appearance of Christ, after which all the Jews present accept Christianity.[76] It was a topic of Byzantine eschatology that the coming of the Last Emperor would herald the conversion of the Jews in Jerusalem;[77] meanwhile the abjuration formulae were there, ready and waiting, should an immediate need actually arise. They also provided the arguments available for writers to use in other kinds of texts.

It is no accident then that manuscripts that contain abjuration formulae for Muslims also contain equivalent formulae for Jews and Manichaeans and other "heresies," or that strings of anathemas are followed by an exposition of orthodoxy. A broadly similar pattern is followed, if at far greater length, in Manuel II's *Dialogues with a Persian*, as also in Kydones, and in the so-called dialogues on Islam by the Emperor John VI Cantacuzenus (d. 1383).[78]

Jews and Muslims: the same but different

Despite their many similarities, the conditions that produced the dialogues and other texts against Jews and those against Muslims were not symmetrical. In the case of the anti-Jewish works there is also a difference between the Latin and the Greek texts. In the twelfth-century west, the role of Jews was seen in terms of "service"—for their witness in the Hebrew Scriptures and their alleged blindness, by which the truth of Christianity was demonstrated. This was essentially the position of Augustine, and so far as Byzantium was concerned, while Augustine was better known than some have thought, it was for his Trinitarian arguments, rather than for the full range of his writings where his position on Jews manifested itself.[79] Augustine's "hermeneutical Jew," not based, it seems, on much acquaintance with real living Jews, gave Jews a special status, for ever to be preserved but for ever subordinate. Many Byzantine writers also found the dialogical or hermeneutical Jew a useful trope, but important as this Augustinian legacy was for western medieval writers on the subject, in their dialogues against Jews Byzantines drew on their own long-established *Adversus Iudaeos* tradition. Many scholars have also written about the perilous situation of Jews in the medieval west, and asked about its connection with other forms of persecution. All I would say now (with caution) is that the hermeneutical Jew in Byzantium served somewhat different ends, and perhaps also worked differently in Byzantium itself than, for example, in south Italy.[80]

Byzantine *Adversus Iudaeos* texts were intimately connected with the cognitive expression of orthodoxy and heresy, and in the case of anti-Muslim texts in Byzantium, too, Islam was usually constructed, in a cognitive exercise of Christian self-definition, whether as a perversion of Christianity and so in principle capable of responding to reasoned debate, or as a version of paganism only to be confronted with polemic.[81] Christian-Jewish and Christian-Muslim texts in Greek are rarely discussed together in the context of social or cultural history. While it would be premature to rush to conclusions it seems that despite the interest shown by Manuel I, the engagement of Byz-

antium with the Muslim world on so many different and urgent levels did not often include the aim
of acquiring reliable information about their religion.
This may seem surprising in view of the penetration
of the Seljuks in Anatolia and the complicated ways in
which the Byzantines dealt with this. On the ground
relations could be pragmatic: Alexius I was happy to
rely on the aid of a Turk, Sulayman, against his own
rivals, and to use him as his deputy in western Anatolia to control the Turks and supply troops for Alexius to use against the Normans, even, it seems, to en-
trust to him the key city of Nicaea.[82] He also turned
to Sulayman to recover Antioch after the Byzantine
general Philaretos had gone over to the other side and
converted to Islam.[83] After this beginning, however,
Turkish control in Anatolia increased apace and Alexius's policy of alliances came to nothing. There was
concern in Constantinople for the threat to episcopal sees in Anatolia. But when a Latin patriarch of
Antioch was established by the crusaders, and John
the Oxite exiled to Constantinople, the latter occupied himself with writing against Latins rather than
with Islam.

The arrival of western crusaders in the east in the
late eleventh century meant that Byzantines, Turks
and Latins were operating in the same geographical
arena. Yet how much actual debate there was in Con-

131

stantinople about religious differences with Islam is unclear, certainly in comparison with the constant discussion of the issues dividing the Latin and Greek churches. While there had been a mosque in Constantinople since the tenth century, if not earlier, serving the needs of Muslim prisoners, traders and visitors, Muslims in the city seem as yet to have formed a "floating population" rather than a settled community parallel to the Jewish one; references to a Muslim quarter are later in date.[84] As Vera von Falkenhausen points out, anti-Jewish dialogues are far commoner than anti-Muslim ones, and Magdalino also remarks that the twelfth century produced "hardly any polemic against the greatest adversary of all, Islam," concluding that there was no need for further argument: Christian conversion to Islam was simply unthinkable.[85] We also saw that when the Byzantine anti-Muslim texts seek to refute accusations against Christian doctrine in the Qur'ān or in *hadith*, they resort to inventions and fanciful accusations. Yet provincials in parts of Anatolia rubbed shoulders with Muslim Turks, or were ruled by them.

By the thirteenth century, after 1204 and with the increasing fragmentation of Mediterranean society, one might expect more real engagement with Islam. In 1355, St Gregory Palamas wrote about the Turks who had captured him and his companions when their ship got into difficulties off Gallipoli. According to his own account Palamas was ordered by Orhan to debate with Muslim theologians, and the debate was recorded by the Sultan's Greek physician, Taronites. He also debated with a group he calls the Chiones at Orhan's summer resort about the divinity of Christ, the resurrection, the nature of God, circumcision, and the Mosaic law. In Nicaea soon afterwards he discussed Christianity with an imam at the monastery of Hyacinthus after watching a Muslim funeral.[86] But in earlier periods we are more likely to find writers treating the themes of Jews and Muslims instrumentally. In doing so they were defending orthodoxy as they saw it. "Thinking with Jews" and "thinking with Islam" were both embedded in the Byzantine consciousness as tools of religious definition.

Classification and taxonomy

Like the dialogues and debates between Latins and Greeks considered in chapter two, those between Christians and Jews and Christians and Muslims represent modes of taxonomy or types of classification. In this they resemble and draw on the examples set by the massive literature setting out taxonomies of heresy. Details and background may differ in individual

133

cases, but taken together they represent repeated attempts to define social norms—which is not of course to say that they succeeded in producing definitive statements. Some of the texts I have discussed sprang from official initiatives, but this was not always the case, and it is a mistake to regard them collectively as the product of an official church. According to Mary Douglas, institutions impose classifications.[87] In the Byzantine case authority and initiative were alike dispersed. Nonetheless they had a powerful collective effect on the articulation of thought in this society.

To be sure, the Christian-Jewish dialogues can sometimes provide hints about the real relations of Christians and Jews. But even more importantly for my present argument, they played an instrumental role within Byzantine society.[88] Taxonomies can and do take many forms; the subject in these cases is religion, the most powerful cognitive principle in medieval society. I argued earlier for the inclusion of Christian theological and "religious" examples in the broader study of Byzantine dialogue and debate, and the same applies also to the dialogues and treatises dealing with Jews and Muslims. Retrieving these works from the technical field of modern scholarship known as theology, to which they are usually relegated by literary scholars, and bringing them into the mainstream of historical and literary critique, opens

134

up a large category of material often too readily dismissed by non-theologians. Above all it has the advantage of making them available for an analysis in terms of the discursive practices in Byzantine society as a whole.

Can the apparently highly specialized anti-Latin, anti-Jewish and anti-Muslim discourses that have been my subject here and in the last chapter be connected with the high-style literary productions considered in chapter one? At first sight they seem miles apart. Can any of this be knitted together into a more integrated historical sociology of the period? That is the challenge, and I will set out some ideas about it in the Conclusions that follow.

135

Conclusions

Bringing it Together

The dialogues that have been the theme of these three chapters cover an immense range of subject matter and type, from the highly literary and the philosophical to the seemingly very different dialogues between Christians and Jews or Muslims, for which there had been many precedents already. Tying them together into some kind of overarching literary explanation seems impossible, if not indeed misguided. Yet they are united by their overall form and dialogic nature, and they all belong in the long tradition of dialogue composition in Greek since the early Christian period that continued until and even beyond the end of Byzantium. In western Europe, meanwhile, the rise of disputation gave rise to huge numbers of dialogue texts in Latin, and was later succeeded by an enormous flourishing of dialogue in the Renaissance and after.[1] Our dialogues are part of a long history that began in classical Greece and is part of the history of

Europe. All the more reason then not to neglect the large number of Byzantine examples, or to limit attention to the more "literary" among them—something that we can hardly afford to do in any case, given the uncertainty that still surrounds the whole question of what counts as "literary" in Byzantium.[2]

Writing in the dialogue form necessarily involves ventriloquism, speaking in the persona of another, and in this huge mass of writing the authorial voice often escapes us, especially among the more literary twelfth-century dialogues that do receive discussion, and even though the twelfth century seems to have been an age of increasing authorial self-assertion. It is true that hiding behind the dialogue form could be seen as a "masking" process whereby the author could experiment and defer commitment. But dialogues could also lead as clearly to certain conclusions as do Socrates's answers in the later dialogues of Plato. There is evidently much to be done in terms of the analysis of the dialogic elements in these Byzantine works.[3] In particular we need at this stage to look at individual examples on their own terms, especially since so many still remain without good editions or critical studies, part of the great submerged body of material that is Byzantine literature.

In chapter one I referred to two prominent themes in current scholarship on the literary production of the eleventh and twelfth centuries, namely performance and competition, and I want to return to them now. Both terms are applied by modern scholars in a narrow sense, to refer to the fact that the *literati* of Constantinople literally performed their compositions in select social gatherings of equals, or potential equals. Equally, individuals competed with each other for patronage, for positions and for fame, and schools competed against each other in agonistic displays. But let us see if we can extend and broaden the application of both these terms.

Dialogues of the more literary kind could indeed be envisaged by their authors in dramatic terms; we have seen this in the case of Anselm of Havelberg, and a good case has been made for this conscious theatricality in the later dialogues of Cicero.[4] However there is also another sense in which the term "performance" can be used, and here I turn again to scholarship on late antiquity.[5] In this sense "performance" refers not to the actual performance of a literary work, that is, its oral delivery, or to the sense of "theatre" in Byzantine culture, or to the "performativity" of a text, but to the performance, in the sense of the establishment or projection, of a persona, an identity, or a set of ideas. Literary production, in twelfth-century Byzantium as in fourth- and fifth-century late antiquity, was very much a matter of the performance of *paideia*, which

139

itself constituted a form of cultural or social capital and was essential to personal as well as literary success. This went alongside a high level of scholarly activity addressed to the classical literary works that lay at the basis of *paideia*.[6] Everyone, including emperors, understood what was required, and how things worked. Being a *pepaideumenos* ("possessor of *paideia*," a term also applied to the *literati* of the twelfth century) was not a status reached by all, even among the elite: it was a recognized status, open only to the best, and according to generally accepted rules. The "professional" writers of twelfth-century Byzantium knew that and took it to heart. As for late antiquity, in a recent discussion of Greek high-style culture in the fourth century, Lieve Van Hoof has written that "Greek culture was not a fossilized set of ready-made topoi" but needed to be performed, that is, expressed and conceived, in such a way that others recognized the performance.[7] Another discussion on the subject of Hellenism in the late antique period that includes texts by Christian authors (termed "Christian sophists"), talks about performance in similar terms: rather than being a given, in essentialist terms, "Hellenism" was a "rhetorical and conceptual toolbox," available to be used by would-be *pepaideumenoi* or *literati*.[8] The author, Aaron Johnson, is writing about just the kind of Hellenism also practised by literary aspirants in the twelfth century, and his list of "tools" suits them very well: they include a learned language (or "sociolect"), citation of or allusion to classical authors, use of rhetorical figures and structures, invented classicizing characters, and, most interestingly for us now, "generic, conceptual categories for classifying the world"; According to Johnson Hellenism is "an aggregate'" of various elements, not a simple given. The argument has been well put for Michael Psellus in the eleventh century by Papaioannou and could be developed further for twelfth-century texts.[9] I would argue that the same applies to the "performance of orthodoxy," a term I borrow from Virginia Burrus and others and which is applied to Byzantine liturgical expression by Derek Krueger.[10]

The question of Hellenism is highly relevant for my discussion, in a period when Byzantines started to call themselves Hellenes again.[11] But discussions of Hellenism sometimes confuse national and ethnic issues with that of classicising culture. Similarly "identity" covers many more nuances than these. I would like to dwell on the last element in the list given above, namely, the assertion of "generic, conceptual categories for classifying the world,"[12] and to focus on the processes of cognition. However it was conceived or claimed, "Hellenism" needed to be constructed and articulated, and high-style literary production, whether secular or Christian, was the prime way of achieving this

141

construction. Again, the Second Sophistic can be instructive. While most modern writers on the Second Sophistic movement in the early Roman empire—itself a model for the writers of our twelfth-century period—avoid considering Christian texts, a welcome recent discussion by Kendra Eshleman rightly argues that Christian writers also shared in that movement towards fashioning a Hellenic identity.[13] There are many similarities and also many differences between twelfth-century literary culture and the world of the Second Sophistic. In our period we do not have the complicating factor of the need for the kind of Christian apologetic that was needed in the early centuries, or the same tension between Christian and pagan. Nor were poets and the authors of secular high-style texts the only *pepaideumenoi* in Middle Byzantium. As the dialogues show, many of the authors of religious works also possessed and demonstrated *paideia*. But the sharing of a common intellectual and literary environment by Christian and non-Christian writers seen by Eshleman for the Second Sophistic is surely also true for the twelfth century and for both explicitly Christian and apparently secular works—which, as we have seen, were often written by the same authors. A new dimension was opened up in our present period with the impact of westerners in the period of the Crusades and the growing assertion of the papacy, and this made the

142

asseration of a specifically Byzantine *paideia* even more critical.

What we see so vividly in this period—and this is not surprising—is an intense and multi-faceted effort to find definition. Comnenian Constantinople was indeed caught between several challenges: pressure at once political, military and religious, from the west and the problems caused by the growing presence and increasing dominance of the Turks in the traditional Byzantine homelands of Asia Minor. These combined with internal religious controversy, with emperors attempting to play a central role, but not always succeeding, and not least the social tensions surrounding the embedding of a dynasty that had come to power by a coup and still needed to control the rivalries that ensued.[14] The social upheaval resulting from the establishment of the Comnenian dynasty in 1081 followed only ten years after the defeat and capture of an emperor by the Seljuks at Manzikert in the east, and the loss of Bari, the Byzantine stronghold in southern Italy, to the Normans in the same year. As well as their tense relations with the crusaders the Comnenian emperors were also forced to spend much of their time in the effort to win back or consolidate their lost territories. In addition, Alexius I Comnenus imposed a dramatically different hierarchy and a new style of administration, thereby also

143

creating entirely new forms of competition and rivalry. Education and literary production shared in this (though recent publications have made it clear that it was an eleventh- as well as a twelfth-century phenomenon). Nor was the level of competition confined to the new aristocracy. In terms of stability, Byzantium was lucky to have two long-reigning emperors in Alexius I and Manuel I, who were able to weather the storms of a highly unstable political system. It was a society and a culture of an elite, even if not strictly of an aristocracy. But such was the internal upheaval within twelfth-century society that it could also produce a writer like the "poor" Prodromos, who took advantage of these divisions by expressing himself in a different sociolect and producing "begging" poems complaining of his ordinary background, his poverty and his misfortune.[15]

Twelfth-century literature emerged in a situation both of opportunity and of anxious competitiveness and jostling for position, in fact in the context of a classic case of elite formation, at a time when Byzantium was challenged by multiple external and indeed internal threats.[16] Education and literary production provided the arena in which this competitiveness was exercised, and both the oral performances at which writers exposed their new work and the competitions between schools were the occasions on which it was showcased and judged. Written compositions, including dialogues, were part of that, and I suggest that we read the dialogues and debates against the Latins, Armenians and heterodox Byzantines, as well as Jews and Muslims, in the same way.

In Lyons in 1274 and at Ferrara/Florence in 1438–39 Byzantines and westerners reached agreements about church union, but in both cases the result divided the Byzantine side. Less than two decades after leading the Byzantine return to Constantinople, Michael VIII Palaeologus became the focus of bitter opposition at home and even of personal anathemas for his pro-Latin policy. Despite harsh treatment meted out to his opponents his hoped-for union did not stick. Like others before and after him the patriarch John Bekkos changed sides more than once, but ended by being again a powerful opponent of union. A hundred and fifty or so years later, the proceedings of the Council of Ferrara/Florence occupied many months of detailed research and preparation, but despite all the efforts made by the then emperor and his massive entourage its conclusions split the Byzantine side again and several leading Byzantines converted to Roman Catholicism. This longstanding and painful argument produced only recurring and difficult division.

In the twelfth century, as we saw, numerous debates took place about the possibility of union. One question is how far the written texts that we have actually represent what was said. But another, from the Byzantine side, is their role in constructing the Latin position. Like the lists of Latin "errors," these records of public proceedings and these literary compositions with their binary oppositions between Latins and Greeks constructed western Christianity according to hostile lines, and acted as performances of the divide between western and eastern Christianity. As for the westerners, though they were called barbarians and heretics by Anna Comnena,[17] they were linked to a Roman papacy that itself had entered a new phase, and that threatened the cherished Romanness of Byzantium. Pro-Latin imperial policies in twelfth-century Byzantium made the situation even more complex.

The challenge operated on many levels. The new practice of disputation in the west itself constituted a performance culture, and with its claims to be based on reason it directly challenged traditional Byzantine ways of thought and their reliance on arguments based on authority.[18] The appeal to reason, in fact a highly emotional claim, that is a feature in Latin works of the period found its counterpart in the Byzantine compositions where we find instead a condemnation of logic against tradition, even as authors themselves also relied on syllogisms and Aristotelian logic and criticised their western opponents precisely for arguing contentiously and without the necessary formal equipment. The challenge from the Latins went very deep into Byzantine consciousness and played itself out over several difficult centuries. Drawing on his closeness to the Pisan Hugo Eteriano, the Emperor Manuel I sought to find a way of rapprochement. But despite his efforts, anti-Latin debates and dialogues, replaying arguments on the same theme rehearsed many times already, acted as the mechanism whereby sterotyped conceptions of the "Latins" were performed, driven home and reinforced.

It was no different with internal religious disputes. The twelfth-century modifications to the *Synodikon of Orthodoxy* amounted to a public performance of official orthodoxy, as also did the posting up in Hagia Sophia of Manuel I's edict in 1166. Dialogues composed with the aim of demonstrating orthodoxy, like that of Soterichos Panteugenos, were presumably actually performed, and in any case had the same effect. Orthodoxy, as in the great compendia of Zigabenus, Kamateros and Niketas Choniates, was performed as much as it was argued for, whether in these texts or in the actual performances of the liturgy.[19] That the formulations these works contained were still constantly challenged made the performance all the more necessary. Performing, rather than guarding, orthodoxy, is what we see in these challenging years.

147

Turning to the Byzantine approach to Jews and Muslims, we can make a similar argument. Appeal has been made to the utility of the hermeneutical or dialogical Jew in the history of Christian and western thought.[20] Jews were the subject of fiercely hostile rhetoric in the twelfth-century west, and at times of actual persecution. But they were also "good to think with," and the same applies to the ideological role that Jews continued to play in Byzantium. Jews and Judaism also "worked," that is, served a purpose, for Byzantine thinkers and writers.

Greek texts against Islam in the Byzantine period had a long history even if they lacked the even longer resonances of the *Adversus Iudaeos* literature. But unlike the case with Jews and Judaism, the need to refute the claims of Islam in the Comnenian period was linked to a real military threat, and the Greek anti-Muslim works incorporated elements of direct polemic. In both cases Byzantine authors worried about and hoped for the possibility of the conversion, but Muslims were the "other" in a different sense from Jews.[21]

It is my contention that the various writings I have discussed in these chapters, so disparate at first sight, must be taken together in order to give an insight into the cognitive and therefore the social world of the twelfth century, the same world that gave rise to the burst of literary activity and complex cultural life of the period. The Greek anti-Muslim and anti-Jewish texts alike are intimately connected with Christian anti-heretical compositions; equally, they are inextricably bound up with the cognitive and intellectual concerns of the period that also gave rise to the flowering of other sorts of literature. These works, like the debates and dialogues on the *Filioque* and other issues of disagreement between the Latins and Greeks, with their seemingly formulaic and repetitive lists of arguments, their concern for classification and the cumulative effect that it was evidently hoped they would have, evoke anthropological and sociological parallels. It seems obvious to associate them with identity-formation, as indeed has been done. Yet we must be careful not to simplify. In her book challengingly entitled *How Institutions Think* the social anthropologist Mary Douglas set out a powerful argument for the cognitive impact of institutions on individuals and society.[22] In this sense institutions, of whatever kind, create identity through collective representations; further, the identity thus created may be of many different kinds, according to the institution or the group that is active in this way. In this analysis religion is not necessarily seen as "a church," something separate or inherently different from other social communities. In twelfth-century Byzantine culture religious attitudes were an integral component in the collective representations engendered by the elite group

149

of *literati* and would-be *literati* who produced the dialogues considered here. But the Byzantine "church" was not a highly structured single institution and orthodoxy was subject to performance and construction just as much as *paideia*. Conceptions of orthodoxy also differed, and had to be constantly re-asserted.

Some of our dialogues emanated, as we have seen, from staged confrontational occasions, and many such occasions are known from the period on which I have concentrated. They required a good deal of preparation and planning, and they involved the interplay of two or more different characters, with an audience to persuade. The written versions of such debates, however far from what may actually have been said, were themselves cast in this essentially dramatic form. But choosing to cast a philosophical or other argument in the style of a dialogue is also essentially to present it in a dramatic form in which individual characters assume and perform in contrasting *personae*. It is not clear that this dramatic element went as far in Byzantium as it did on occasion in German passion plays of the fourteenth and fifteenth centuries,[23] by which time the Jewish characters have become crude stock caricatures, but the very form of dialogue enabled the interplay of characters and arguments. Dialogues permitted what has been called "transparency and dissimulation," allowing insights into the actual differences that lay beneath apparent sameness.[24] However much the authors aimed in their dialogues to construct orthodoxy or articulate right responses in conflict situations, by using the dialogue form they also allowed their audiences to see under the mask.

Although dialogues had been composed in Byzantium for centuries, dialogue was also a supremely suitable mode of expression at a time when society was changing. Dialogue is essentially ambivalent; it allows a questioning and an internal conversation to which other discursive modes are less open. Even in the case of the dialogues against heretics, Jews and Muslims, which seem so obviously designed to construct the "other," sensitivity to differentiation can reveal a less monolithic view.[25] The authors of dialogues and their characters alike present themselves in the works as they simulate and perform the positions for which they argue, and the persuasiveness of their performance depends on the rhetorical skill with which they can persuade us that they are speaking the truth.

To conclude

There is widespread current agreement that Byzantine discursive culture in the long twelfth century, and before the rupture of 1204, relied on performance and

151

on competition. I have tried to broaden that assessment by focusing on one literary form, the dialogue, and by widening its scope to include types of writing and subject matter that do not usually feature in the lively current scholarship on Byzantine literature in the period. The assessment thus takes us beyond the narrowly "literary" and into a much broader conception of the discursive. It focuses admittedly on the literary production of the urban elite and of the educated class, yet, I would argue, this is no bad place to start.

It may seem obvious to suggest that literary and written production in relation to heresy, Judaism and Islam, as well as Christian orthodoxy and indeed Hellenism, was deeply engaged in the construction of an "other," whatever that may be in the particular circumstances. However, the twelfth century also presents prime material for cultural hybridity.[26] Cognitive challenges abounded, from dealing with the west and with Latin Christianity to renewed self-consciousness about Hellenism, continuing issues about what did and did not count as orthodox, familiar themes relating to Jews and Judaism (always good to think with) and more immediate ones about relations with Muslims in Asia Minor and further east. Finally, these challenges were clearly reflected in the struggle of the emerging *literati* and intellectuals to find appropriate cultural expression.

152

Dialogues seem to me to be a particularly useful way of looking at all of this. Not only can the form be used in many different ways, but it is also inherently argumentative and suited to presenting a case or an issue—as some Byzantine writers themselves point out. Not only are dialogues essentially performative, in the sense in which the term is current in reference to Byzantine literature; they are also extremely well suited for the performance of elite literary culture, as for that of orthodoxy, as well as for reactions to Latin Christianity and to Judaism and Islam, and for the philosophical questions that were also being debated in these elite circles.

I have tried to show through this lens that the overall literary production of the long twelfth century in Byzantium is far from being understood as yet, and in particular that the theological part of it is far from uniform, and far more complex than terms like "fortress mentality" or "retreat into an impasse"[27] suggest.

Can we therefore use these dialogues and these perceptions in order to build up a better and more fruitful way of looking at the Byzantine cultural matrix in the twelfth century? I would answer, like President Obama, yes we can.

Notes

Preface

1 Miri Rubin, *Emotion and Devotion: The Meaning of Mary in Medieval Religious Cultures*, The Natalie Zemon Davis Annual Lectures (Budapest–New York: Central European University Press, 2009), 79.

Introduction

1 See Panagiotis Roilos, *Amphoteroglossia: A Poetics of the Twelfth-Century Medieval Greek Novel* (Washington, DC: Center for Hellenic Studies, 2005), and see Elizabeth M. Jeffreys, "The Comnenian Background to the *romans de l'antiquité*," *Byzantion* 50 (1980): 455–86 (repr. in Elizabeth Jeffreys and Michael Jeffreys, *Popular Literature in Late Byzantium* [London: Variorum, 1983], no. X) and Panagiotis A. Agapitos, "In Rhomaian, Frankish and Persian Lands: Fiction and Fictionality in Byzantium," in *Medieval Narrative between History and Fiction: From the Centre to the Periphery of Europe, c. 1100–1400*, ed. Panagiotis A. Agapitos and Lars Boje Mortensen (Copenhagen: Museum Tusculanum Press, 2012), 235–367. On narrativity and the Comnenian "novels" see Ingela Nilsson, *Raconter Byzance. La littérature au XIIe siècle* (Paris: Les Belles Lettres, 2014), 39–86, with Panagiotis A. Agapitos and Dieter Reinsch, *Der Roman im Byzanz in*

der Komnenenzeit (Frankfurt am Main: Beerenverlag, 2000). English translations of all four: Elizabeth Jeffreys, *Four Byzantine Novels* (Liverpool: Liverpool University Press, 2012).

2   For this see Floris Bernard, *Writing and Reading Byzantine Secular Poetry, 1025–81* (New York: Oxford University Press, 2014), with *Poetry and its Contexts in Eleventh-Century Byzantium*, ed. Floris Bernard and Kristoffel Demoen (Farnham: Ashgate, 2012).

3   Ruth Macrides and Paul Magdalino, "The Fourth Kingdom and the Rhetoric of Hellenism," in *The Perception of the Past in Twelfth-Century Europe*, ed. Paul Magdalino (London: Hambledon, 1992), 117–55, provide a useful introduction to the secular literary output of the period.

4   Anthony Kaldellis, "The Byzantine Role in the Making of the Corpus of Classical Greek Historiography: A Preliminary Investigation," *JHS* 132 (2012): 74.

5   For Anna as patron of this group see Peter Frankopan, "The Literary, Cultural and Philosophical Context for the Twelfth-Century Commentary on the Nicomachean Ethics," in Charles Barber and David Jenkins, eds., *Medieval Greek Commentaries on the Nicomachean Ethics* (Leiden: Brill, 2009), 45–62; doubts are expressed by Michele Trizio, "From Anna Komnene to Dante: The Byzantine Roots of Western Debates about Aristotle's *Nicomachean Ethics*," in *Dante and the Greeks*, ed. Jan Ziolkowsky (Washington, DC: Dumbarton Oaks, 2015), 105–39.

6   Anna's work is the subject of a recent study by Penelope Buckley, *The Alexiad of Anna Komnene: Artistic Strategy in the Making of Myth* (Cambridge: Cambridge University Press, 2014), as well as a collection of essays edited by Thalia Gouma-Peterson, *Anna Komnene and Her Times* (New York: Garland Publishing, 2000), and see the Penguin translation, revised by Peter Frankopan with a useful introduction (2009).

7   Women patrons included the *sebastokratorissa* Irene, on whom see Elizabeth M. Jeffreys, "The Sebastokratorissa Irene as Patron," in *Female Founders in Byzantium and Beyond*, ed. Lioba Theis, Margaret Mullett, Michael Grünbart, Galina Fingarova and Matthew Savage (Köln-Weimar-Wien: Böhlau Verlag, 2014), 177–94; other candidates

156

include the ex-*basilissa* Maria, wife of Alexius I's deposed predecessor, Alexius's mother, Anna Dalassena, and his wife, Irene Doukaina: see Margaret Mullett, "Aristocracy and Patronage in the Literary Circles of Comnenian Constantinople," in *The Byzantine Aristocracy, IX to XIII Centuries*, ed. Michael Angold (Oxford: B.A.R., 1984), 173–201. Learned Byzantine women are also discussed by Maria Mavroudi, "Learned Women of Byzantium and the Surviving Record," in *Byzantine Religious Culture: Studies in Honor of Alice-Mary Talbot*, ed. Denis Sullivan, Elizabeth Fisher and Stratis Papaioannou (Leiden: Brill, 2012), 53–84.

8   See the overview by Margaret Mullett, one of the pioneers in this field, "Epistolography," in Elizabeth M. Jeffreys, with John Haldon and Robin Cormack, ed., *The Oxford Handbook of Byzantine Studies* (Oxford: Oxford University Press, 2008), 882–93, and on twelfth-century letters and social networks, Michael Grünbart, "'Tis Love that has Warm'd us': Reconstructing Networks in 12th Century Byzantium," *Revue belge de philologie et d'histoire* 83.2 (2005): 301–13.

9   Bernard, *Writing and Reading*; Stratis Papaioannou, *Michael Psellos: Rhetoric and Authorship in Byzantium* (Cambridge: Cambridge University Press, 2013).

10   For their problems see Margaret Mullett, "Whose Muses? Two Advice Poems attributed to Alexios I Komnenos," in *La face cachée de la littérature byzantine. Le texte en tant que message immédiat: Actes du colloque international, Paris, 5–6–7 juin 2008, organisé par Paolo Odorico en mémoire du Constantin Leventis*, ed. Paolo Odorico. Dossiers byzantins 11 (Paris: Centre d'études byzantines, néo-helléniques et sud-ouest européennes, École des Hautes Études en Sciences Sociales, 2012), 195–220.

11   Though this does not make twelfth-century Byzantium into a theocracy, as claimed by Buckley, *The Alexiad of Anna Komnene*, 19–23.

12   For instance fifty-six exercises known as *progymnasmata* and twenty-six personifications (*ethopoiiai*) survive by Nikephoros Basilakes, from the 1130s or 1140s: Papaioannou, *Michael Psellos*, 147; Nilsson, *Raconter Byzance*, 145–52, 200–201. Basilakes had a notable ecclesiastical career and held the post of *didaskalos* of the Apostle: Michael An-

gold, *Church and Society under the Comneni 1081–1261* (Cambridge: Cambridge University Press, 1995), 79–80, 90–91, 173. Contests in "schedography," an innovation of the later eleventh century in which a teacher would comment in detail on a short passage, are described by Bernard, *Writing and Reading*, 259–66.

13 Elizabeth M. Jeffreys,"We Need to Talk about Byzantium: or, Byzantium, its Reception of the Classical World as Discussed in Current Scholarship, and Should Classicists Pay Attention?," *Classical Receptions Journal* 6.1 (2014), 158–74; see also for poetry ead.,"Why produce Verse in Twelfth-Century Constantinople?," in *Doux remède –: poésie et poétique à Byzance*, ed. Paolo Odorico, Panagiotis A. Agapitos and Martin Hinterberger, Dossiers byzantins 9 (Paris: Centre d'études byzantines, néo-helléniques et sud-ouest européennes, École des Hautes Études en Sciences Sociales, 2008), 219–28.

14 Nilsson, *Raconter Byzance*, 11–38.

15 A short but useful survey exists by Anna Ieraci Bio, "Il dialogo nella letteratura bizantina," in *Spirito e forma della letteratura bizantina: Actes de la séance plénière d'ouverture du XXe Congrès international des études byzantines, Paris, 19–25 août, 2001*, ed. Antonio Garzya (Naples: Quaderni dell'accademia pontaniana 47, 2006), 21–45; there is some Byzantine material in Mario Coppola, Germana Fernicola and Lucia Pappalardo, eds., *Dialogus. Il dialogo fra le religioni nel pensiero tardo-antico, medievale e umanistico* (Rome: Città Nuova, 2014), for which I am grateful to Alberto Rigolio. More has been written on dialogues from the late antique period, but again much less than the subject deserves—I have given a preliminary overview in *Dialoguing in Late Antiquity*, Hellenic Studies 65 (Washington, DC: Center for Hellenic Studies, 2014). For dialogues post-Plato see now Sandrine Dubel and Sophie Gotteland, eds., *Formes et genres du dialogue antique*, Scripta Antiqua 71 (Bordeaux: Éditions Ausonius, 2015). For Aristotelian, Ciceronian and Augustinian dialogues see also Vittorio Hösle, *The Philosophical Dialogue* (Notre Dame, Ind.: University of Notre Dame Press, 2012), 82–98, though Hösle's focus is on the west and does not include discussion of the Byzantine dialogues.

16 For instance on closer inspection Theodore Prodromos's *Bion prasis* is

158

not as straightforwardly indebted to Lucian as has been assumed (see below).

17 Some are addressed in my "Thinking with Byzantium," *Transactions of the Royal Historical Society* 21 (2011), 39–57, and *Byzantine Matters* (Princeton: Princeton University Press, 2014).

Chapter 1

1   I have discussed this episode in Cameron, *Byzantine Matters*, chap. 5, and for the renewed debate about religious images see Charles Barber, *Contesting the Logic of Painting: Art and Understanding in Eleventh-Century Byzantium* (Leiden: Brill, 2007), 93–130. The Greek text of the dialogue is published in A. Demetrakopoulos, *Ekklesiastike Bibliotheke* I (Leipzig: Othon Bigandos, 1866; reprint Hildesheim: Olms, 1965), 128–51, but there is no modern edition.

2   Eustratius and his commentary are discussed in several of the contributions to Barber and Jenkins, eds., *Medieval Greek Commentaries*; he also drew on the Neoplatonist Proclus, as shown by Michele Trizio, "Neoplatonic Source-Material in Eustratios of Nicaea's Commentary on Book VI of the Nicomachean Ethics," in Barber and Jenkins, eds., *Medieval Greek Commentaries*, 71–109.

3   The indispensable work is Paul Magdalino's *The Empire of Manuel I Komnenos, 1143–1180* (Cambridge: Cambridge University Press, 1993), which ranges considerably more widely than the date range suggests; in what follows my debt to it is obvious even where I may disagree.

4   Athanasios Markopoulos, "Teachers and Textbooks in Byzantium, Ninth to Eleventh Centuries," in *Networks of Learning: Perspectives on Scholars in Byzantine East and Latin West c. 1000–1200*, ed. Sita Steckel, Niels Gaul and Michael Grünbart (Berlin and Münster: LIT Verlag, 2014), 3–16.

5   Markopoulos, "Teachers and Textbooks," 9.

6   There is no overall guide to all these dialogues, but for a collection of studies see Averil Cameron and Niels Gaul, eds., *Dialogues and Debates from Late Antiquity to Late Byzantium* (forthcoming); especially

George Karamanolis, "Form and Content in the Dialogues of Genna-dios Scholarios," and for the late antique period Cameron, *Dialoguing*. A handlist of Greek and Syriac dialogues from the second century to c. 600 is in preparation by Alberto Rigolio.

7 For these see Roberto Romano, ed., *La satira bizantina dei secoli XI–XV: Il patriota, Caridemo, Timarione, Cristoforo di Mitilene, Michele Psello, Theodoro Prodromo, Carmi ptocoprodromici, Michele Haplu-cheir, Giovanni Catrara, Mazaris, La messa del glabro, Sinissario del venerabile asino* (Turin: Unione tipografico editrice torinese, 1999).

8 Inbuilt problems: Paul Stephenson, "Byzantium Transformed, c. 950–1200," *Medieval Encounters* 10 (2004): 185–210; Paul Stephenson, "The Rise of the Middle Byzantine Aristocracy and the Decline of the Imperial State," in *The Byzantine World,* ed. Paul Stephenson (London: Routledge, 2010), 22–33.

9 For instance Angold, ed., *The Byzantine Aristocracy*; Alexander Kazh-dan and Silvia Ronchey, *L'aristocrazia bizantina dal principio dell'XI alla fine del XII secolo* (Palermo: Sellerio, 1997); Paul Magdalino,"Court Society and Aristocracy," in *A Social History of Byzantium*, ed. John F. Haldon (Chichester: Wiley-Blackwell, 2009), 212–32.

10 Magdalino, *The Empire of Manuel I,* 316–412.

11 See Alexander Kazhdan, in collaboration with Simon Franklin, *Studies on Byzantine Literature of the Eleventh and Twelfth Centuries* (Cambridge: Cambridge University Press, 1984).

12 Panagiotis A. Agapitos, "Literary Criticism," in *The Oxford Handbook of Byzantine Studies*, ed. Elizabeth Jeffreys, John F. Haldon and Robin Cormack (Oxford: Oxford University Press, 2009), 77–85.

13 Marc Lauxtermann, *Byzantine Poetry from Pisides to Geometres* (Vienna: Verlag der Österreichischen Akademie der Wissenschaften, 2003), 21; Papaioannou, *Michael Psellos,* 125, 232–49.

14 Margaret Alexiou, *After Antiquity: Greek Language, Myth and Metaphor* (Ithaca, NY: University of Cornell Press, 2002), 96–97. Alexiou's comments come in a chapter titled "New Departures in the Twelfth Century," based on three works: the fantasy dialogue known as the *Timarion* (on which see below), the romance *Hysmene and Hysmenias* and the Ptochoprodromic, or "poor Prodromos" poems. She empha-

sizes the crossovers between different types of work and prefers the term "literary registers." For "littérarité" see Nilsson, *Raconter Byzance*, 17, 40–48.

15 Alexander Kazhdan and Giles Constable, *People and Power in Byzantium: An Introduction to Modern Byzantine Studies* (Washington, DC: Dumbarton Oaks, 1982), 102; Mullett, "Aristocracy and Patronage," 418; Alexander Kazhdan and Ann Wharton Epstein, *Change in Byzantine Culture in the Eleventh and Twelfth Centuries* (Berkeley and Los Angeles: University of California Press, 1985), 130–31; Paul Magdalino, "Cultural Change?: The Context of Byzantine Poetry from Geometres to Prodromos," in Bernard and Demoen, eds., *Poetry and its Contexts*, 22.

16 Anthony Kaldellis, "The Corpus of Byzantine Historiography: An Interpretive Essay," in Stephenson, ed., *The Byzantine World*, 220.

17 For the latter see Aglae Pizzone, ed., *The Author in Middle Byzantine Literature: Models, Functions and Identities*, Byzantinisches Archiv 28 (Berlin: De Gruyter, 2014); a projected *Oxford Handbook of Byzantine Literature* promises a first chapter on "What is Byzantine literature?"

18 She describes her own trajectory, within the general historiographical trends since World War II, in "Decentering History: Local Stories and Cultural Crossings in a Global World," *History and Theory* 50 (2011): 188–202.

19 So Macrides and Magdalino, "The Fourth Kingdom."

20 Kaldellis, "The Corpus of Byzantine Historiography," 213–15.

21 Lieve Van Hoof and Peter Van Nuffelen, eds., *Literature and Society in the Fourth Century AD: Performing Paideia, Constructing the Present, Presenting the Self* (Leiden: Brill, 2014); see especially Van Hoof and Van Nuffelen, "The Social Role and Place of Literature in the Fourth Century AD," 1–15.

22 Elizabeth A. Clark, *History, Theory, Text: Historians and the Linguistic Turn* (Cambridge, Mass.: Harvard University Press, 2004); I am grateful for access to an unpublished paper by Andrew Jacobs in which this move is described and defended, and see now Elizabeth A. Clark, "The Retrospective Self," *The Catholic Historical Review* 101.1 (2015): 1–27.

161

23 Derek Krueger, ed., *Byzantine Christianity*, People's History of Christianity 3 (Minneapolis, Minn.: Fortress, 2006).

24 John F. Haldon, "Towards a Social History of Byzantium," in Haldon, ed., *A Social History of Byzantium*, 5.

25 John F. Haldon, "The Byzantine Empire," in *The Dynamics of Ancient Empires: State Power from Assyria to Byzantium*, ed. Ian Morris and Walter Scheidel (Oxford: Oxford University Press, 2009), 205–52; compare Walter Scheidel, ed., *Rome and China: Comparative Perspectives on Ancient World Empires* (Oxford: Oxford University Press, 2009).

26 Haldon, "Towards a Social History of Byzantium," 21–30.

27 Ibid.,10.

28 See ibid.,16 for comments on the lack of synthesizing work by Byzantinists.

29 Johann P. Arnason, "Byzantium and Historical Sociology," in Stephenson, ed., *The Byzantine World*, 491–504.

30 Evelyne Patlagean, *Un Moyen Âge grec. Byzance, IXe-XVe siècle* (Paris: Albin Michel, 2007).

31 See Johannes Preiser-Kapeller, "Complex Historical Dynamics of Crisis: The Case of Byzantium," in *Krise und Transformation*, ed. Sigrid Deger-Jalkotzy and Arnold Suppan, Beiträge des internationalen Symposiums vom 22. bis 23. November 2010 an der Österreichischen Akademie der Wissenschaften (Vienna: Verlag der Österreichischen Akademie der Wissenschaften, 2011), 69–128, especially 73–74, 77–86, 87–90.

32 Ibid., 95.

33 See the papers gathered by Johann P. Arnason and Bjorn Wittrock in *Medieval Encounters* 10 (2004), with, for example, R. I. Moore, *The First European Revolution, 950–1215* (Oxford: Blackwell, 2000); intellectual developments in the west and the rise of the medieval disputation technique are discussed in chapter two below.

34 See Niels Gaul, "Rising Elites and Institutionalization – *Ethos/Mores* – 'Debts' and Drafts: Three Concluding Steps towards Comparing Networks of Learning in Byzantium and the 'Latin' West, c. 1000–1200," in Steckel, Gaul and Grünbart, eds., *Networks of Learning*, 235–80.

162

35   Ingela Nilsson writes well about this in "'The Same Story, but An-other': A Reappraisal of Literary Imitation in Byzantium," in *Imitatio – Aemulatio – Variatio*, Akten des internationalen wissenschaftlichen Symposiums zur byzantinischen Sprache und Literatur, Vienna 22–25 octobre 2008, Veröffentlichen zur Byzanzforschung 21, ed. Elisabeth Schiffer and Andreas Rhoby (Vienna: OAW, 2010), 195–208.

36   In general see Michael Grünbart, ed., *Theatron: rhetorische Kultur in Spätantike und Mittelalter* (Berlin: De Gruyter, 2007), and cf. Emmanuel C. Bourbouhakis "Rhetoric and Performance," in Stephenson, ed., *The Byzantine* World, 175–87, and below, Conclusions.

37   Chapter 5, 225–316, in Anthony Kaldellis, *Hellenism in Byzantium: The Transformations of Greek Identity and the Reception of the Classical Tradition* (Cambridge: Cambridge University Press, 2007), is entitled "The Third Sophistic: The Performance of Hellenism under the Komnenoi."

38   For instance see the essays in *Approches de la Troisième Sophistique, Hommages à Jacques Schamp*, ed. Eugenio Amato, with Alexandre Roduit and Martin Steinrück (Brussels: Editions Latomus, 2006); Ryan C. Fowler and Alberto J. Quiroga Puertas, "A Prolegomena to the Third Sophistic," in *Plato in the Third Sophistic*, ed. Ryan C. Fowler (Berlin: De Gruyter, 2014), 1–30. However, disagreement exists as to which authors are to be included.

39   Niels Gaul, *Thomas Magistros und die spätbyzantinische Sophistik. Studien zum Humanismus urbaner Eliten in der frühen Palaiologenzeit*, Mainzer Veröffentlichungen zur Byzantinistik 10 (Wiesbaden: Harrassowitz Verlag, 2011).

40   Alexiou, *After Antiquity*, 98; see also Stephen C. Ferruolo,"The Twelfth-Century Renaissance," in *Renaissances before the Renaissance: Cultural Revivals of Late Antiquity and the Middle Ages*, ed. Warren Treadgold (Stanford: Stanford University Press, 1984), 114–43, with Magdalino, *Empire of Manuel I*, 382–412.

41   Magdalino, *Empire of Manuel I*, 406–408, 392–93; Magdalino, "Cultural Change?" is less gloomy.

42   *Empire of Manuel I*, 408–10, especially 410: Byzantium had no tradition of representative government, and all cultural expression took place "within a framework of doctrinal conformism."

163

43 According to Anthony Kaldellis, "Classical Scholarship in Twelfth-Century Byzantium," in *Medieval Greek Commentaries on the Nicomachean Ethics*, ed. Charles Barber and David Jenkins (Leiden: Brill, 2009), 17, twelfth-century Byzantium was "one of the great ages of Greek rhetoric"; Kaldellis also emphasizes the deep importance attached in these circles to classical scholarship, and the production of a large number of scholia and commentaries.

44 See Martin Hinterberger, *The Language of Byzantine Learned Literature* (Turnhout: Brepols, 2014), for an approach based on linguistics.

45 For the emergence of the Greek vernacular see Michael J. Jeffreys, "The Literary Emergence of Vernacular Greek," *Mosaic* 8.4 (1975): 171–93; Michael J. Jeffreys, "Early Modern Greek Verse: Parallels and Frameworks," *Modern Greek Studies (Australia and New Zealand)* 1 (2012): 49–78.

46 Stratis Papaioannou, "Voice, Signature, Mask: The Byzantine Author," in *The Author in Middle Byzantine Literature: Models, Functions and Identities*, ed. Aglae Pizzone, Byzantinisches Archiv 28 (Berlin: De Gruyter, 2014), 29.

47 Natalie Zemon Davis, *Women on the Margins: Three Seventeenth-Century Lives* (Cambridge, Mass.: Harvard University Press, 1995), 1–4, 5–7.

48 Annelie Volgers and Claudio Zamagni, eds., *Erotapokriseis: Early Christian Question-and-Answer Literature in Context: Proceedings of the Utrecht Colloquium, 13–14 October 2003* (Leuven: Peeters, 2004); Marie-Pierre Bussières, ed., *La littérature des questions et réponses dans l'Antiquité profane et chrétienne: de l'enseignement à l'exégèse: Actes du séminaire sur le genre des questions et réponses tenu à Ottawa les 27 et 28 septembre 2009*, Instrumenta Patristica et Mediaevalia 64 (Turnhout: Brepols, 2011). Some pointers to Byzantine dialogues can be found in the conclusion to my *Dialoguing in Late Antiquity*, 55–58.

49 For the term see Magdalino, *Empire of Manuel I*, 21.

50 English translation by Barry Baldwin, *Timarion* (Detroit: Wayne State University Press, 1984); see recently Anthony Kaldellis, "The *Timarion*: Towards a Literary Description," in Odorico, ed., *La face cachée*, 275–87, developing Kaldellis, *Hellenism*, 276–83.

164

51   G. Miles, "The Representation of Reading in 'Philip the Philosopher,'" *Byzantion* 56 (2009): 292–305.

52   Romano, ed., *La satira bizantina*, 284–335.

53   Margaret Alexiou, "Literary Subversion and the Aristocracy in Twelfth-Century Byzantium: A Stylistic Analysis of the *Timarion*," *BMGS* 8 (1982): 29–45; Dimitris Krallis, "Harmless Satire, Stinging Critique: Notes and Suggestions for Reading the *Timarion*," in *Power and Subversion in Byzantium*, ed. Dimiter Angelov and Michael Saxby (Farnham: Ashgate, 2013), 221–45, making the case for the *Timarion* as a subversive text and endorsed by Alexiou, "Afterword: Literary Subversion in Byzantium," in Angelov and Saxby, eds., *Power and Subversion*, 286.

54   Kaldellis, "The *Timarion*," 275, admitting dialogue at 277 and dissecting the frame dialogue as "subtle dialogic interplay" and with a "Lucianic format" at 278–79.

55   For Theodore as a philosopher see Michele Trizio, "Ancient Physics in the Mid-Byzantine Period: The *Epitome* of Theodore of Smyrna, consul of the philosophers under Alexius I Komnenos (1081–1118)," *Bull. de philosophie médiévale* 58 (2012): 77–99; for Aristotelianism see 82.

56   Psellus dismissed John Italus's rhetorical style as consisting of a collection of syllogisms rather than a stylish argument: Panagiotis Agapitos, "Teachers, Pupils and Imperial Power in Eleventh-century Byzantium," in *Pedagogy and Power: Rhetorics of Classical Learning*, ed. Yun Lee Too and Niall Livingstone (Cambridge: Cambridge University Press, 1998), 184.

57   Przemysław Marciniak, "Theodore Prodromos' *Bion prasis*: A Reappraisal," *GRBS* 53 (2013): 219–39, at 219; see also Tommaso Migliorini, ed., "Gli scritti satirici in greco letterario di Teodoro Prodromo: Introduzione, edizione, traduzione e commenti" (Ph.D diss., University of Pisa, 2010).

58   Barber and Jenkins, eds., *Medieval Greek Commentaries*.

59   I am indebted here to Foteini Spingou.

60   N.G. Charalampopoulos, "A Platonic Dialogue of the Twelfth Century: Theodore Prodromos's *Xenedemos* or *Voices*," *Ariadne* 11 (2005): 189–214 (in Greek).

61   Magdalino, *Empire of Manuel I*, 333.

62   See Kazhdan and Franklin, *Studies on Byzantine Literature*, 87–114.

63   Marciniak, "Theodore Prodromos' *Bion prasis*," 221–24, reacting to the discussion in Christopher Robinson, *Lucian and his Influence in Europe* (London: Duckworth, 1979), 69–73.

64   Marciniak, "Theodore Prodromos' *Bion prasis*," 238.

65   Ed. Herbert Hunger, *Der byzantinische Katz-Mäuse-Krieg* (Graz-Vienna-Cologne: Verlag Böhlau, 1968), arguing for Prodromos as the author.

66   Ed. with Italian translation and commentary by Tommaso Migliorini, "Teodoro Prodromo, *Amaranto*," *MEG* 7 (2007): 183–47; on Lucian, 205–206

67   As argued by Eric Cullhed, "Theodore Prodromos in the Garden of Epicurus," in Cameron and Gaul, eds., *Dialogues and Debates* (forthcoming).

68   Margaret Mullett, "Theophylact of Ohrid's *In Defence of Eunuchs*," in *Eunuchs in Antiquity and Beyond*, ed. Shaun Tougher (London and Swansea, 2002), 180, 184.

69   Charis Messis, "Public hautement affiché et public réellement visé: le cas de *l'Apologie de l'eunuchisme* de Théophylacte d'Achrida," in Odorico, ed., *La face cachée*, 41–85.

70   Among the most recent publications, Pizzone, ed., *The Author in Middle Byzantine Literature*, includes liturgical poetry and hagiography within the purview of the general topic of authorship, though not most other forms of religious or theological writing.

71   Magdalino, *Empire of Manuel I*, 367; compare 369–70, writing of twelfth-century Byzantine intellectuals, "their interest in writing religious literature, and thus, presumably, in reading it or hearing it read, was patently philological"; elsewhere (392) Magdalino concludes that the gap between the "rhetorical theatre" and "the cloister" was real.

72   On which see Eirini Afentoulidou-Leitgeb, "Philippos Monotropos' *Dioptra* and its Social Milieu: Niketas Stethatos, Nikolaos III Grammatikos and the Persecution of Bogomilism," *Parekbolai* 2 (2012): 85–107, and ead.,"The *Dioptra* of Philippos Monotropos: Didactic Verse or Parody?," in Bernard and Demoen, eds., *Poetry and its Contexts*, 181–94.

73 Paul Gautier, "Le *De daemonibus* du Pseudo-Psellos," *REB* 38 (1980): 105–94; Italian trans. by Umberto Albini, *Michele Psello. Sull'attività dei demoni* (Genoa: ECIG, 1985).

74 See chapter two below.

75 Magdalino, *Empire of Manuel I,* 278–79.

76 Magdalino, *Empire of Manuel I,* 279–81; *PG* 140,137–48.

77 Soterichos was accused of syllogizing; see Foteini Spingou, "Dogmatic Disputes in Constantinople: The Dialogue of Soterichos Panteugenos and its Impact," in Cameron and Gaul, eds., *Dialogues and Debates* (forthcoming).

78 For the same problem see Aline Rousselle, "Histoire ancienne et oubli du christianisme (note critique)," *Annales Histoire Sciences Sociales* 47.2 (1992): 355–68.

79 Paul Lemerle, "'Le gouvernement des philosophes': notes et remarques sur l'enseignement, les écoles, la culture," in id., *Cinq études sur le XIe siècle byzantin* (Paris: Éditions du Centre National de Recherché Scientifique, 1977), 195–248.

80 Katerina Ierodiakonou, ed., *Byzantine Philosophy and its Ancient Sources* (Oxford: Oxford University Press, 2002); Börje Bydén and Katerina Ierodiakonou, eds., *The Many Faces of Byzantine Philosophy* (Athens: Norwegian Institute at Athens, 2012).

81 For Alexius see Dion Smythe, "Alexios I and the Heretics: The Account of Anna Komnene's *Alexiad*," in *Alexios I Komnenos I: Papers*, ed. Margaret Mullett and Dion Smythe (Belfast: Belfast Byzantine Enterprises, 1996), 232–59.

82 Robert Browning, "Enlightenment and Repression in Byzantium in the Eleventh and Twelfth Centuries," *Past and Present* 69 (1975): 3–23; cf. Paul Magdalino, "Enlightenment and Repression in the Twelfth Century: The Evidence of the Canonists," in *To byzantio kata ton 12o aiona*, ed. Nicolas Oikonomides (Athens: Hetaireia Vyzantinōn kai Metavyzantinōn Meleton 1991), 357–73; id., "Cultural Change?"; id., *The Empire of Manuel I*, 393; see also Agapitos, "Teachers, Pupils."

83 On the conception of "guardians of Orthodoxy," see also Tia M. Kolbaba, "Byzantines, Armenians, Latins: Unleavened Bread and Heresy in

the Tenth Century," in *Orthodox Constructions of the West*, ed. George E. Demacopoulos and Aristotle Nikolaou (New York: Fordham University Press, 2013), 52–54.

84 Angold, *Church and Society*, 59–60.

85 Cyril Mango, "The Conciliar Edict of 1166," *DOP* 17 (1963): 317–30, with Tia M. Kolbaba, "Byzantine Perceptions of Latin Religious "Errors,'" in *The Crusades from the Perspective of Byzantium and the Muslim World*, ed. Angeliki Laiou and Roy Mottahadeh (Washington, DC: Dumbarton Oaks, 2001), 138–39.

86 Alessandra Bucossi, "The *Sacred Arsenal* by Andronikos Kamateros: A Forgotten Treasure," in *Byzantine Theologians: The Systematization of their own Doctrines and their Perception of Foreign Doctrines*, ed. Antonio Rigo and Pavel Ermilov, Quaderni di "Nea Rhome" 3 (Rome: Università di Roma "Tor Vergata," 2009), 37–38.

87 For such approaches in relation to late antiquity see e.g. Noel Lenski, "Power and Religion on the Frontier of Late Antiquity," in *The Power of Religion in Late Antiquity*, ed. Andrew Cain and Noel Lenski (Farnham: Ashgate, 2009), 1–17; Part I of the volume is subtitled "Religion and the Power of the Word." Ways of seeing: Peter Berger and Thomas Luckmann, *The Social Construction of Reality: A Treatise in the Sociology of Knowledge* (London: Penguin, 1967).

88 Most publications on Niketas Choniates concentrate on his *History*, but for the *Panoply* and its complex and contested reception history see Luciano Bossina, "L'eresia dopo la crociata. Niceta Coniate, i Latini e gli azimi (*Panoplia Dogmatica* XXII," in *Padri Greci e Latini a Confronto (secoli XIII–XV)*, ed. Mariarosa Cortesi (Firenze: SISMEL - Edizioni del Galluzzo, 2004), 154–205, and id, "Niketas Choniates as a Theologian," in *Niketas Choniates: A Historian and a* Writer, ed. Alicia Simpson and Stephanos Efthymiades (Geneva: La Pomme d'Or, 2009), 165–84, with bibliography; further Niccolò Zorzi, "Islam e Cristianesimo durante il regno di Manuele Comneno: la disputa sul 'Dio di Maometto' nell' opera di Niketa Coniata," in *Vie per Bisanzio: VII Congresso Nazionale dell' Associazione Italiana di Studi Bizantini, Venezia, 25–28 novembre, 2009*, ed. Antonio Rigo, Andrea Babuin and Michele Trizio (Bari: Edizioni di Pagina, 2013), 2 vols., I, 275–

310, and see chapters two and three below. The first part of the *Sacred Arsenal* is edited by Alessandra Bucossi, *Andronici Camateri, Sacrum Armamentarium: Pars prima*, Corpus Christianorum Series Graeca 75 (Turnhout: Brepols, 2014); English translation, ead., *Andronicus Camaterus, Sacred Arsenal*, Translated Texts for Byzantinists (Liverpool: Liverpool University Press, in press).

89   *PG* 130. 19-1362.

90   The original presentation copy of the *Sacred Arsenal* does not survive, but the copies of Zigabenus's *Dogmatic* Panoply in Vat. gr. 666 and Mosq. Synod. Gr. 387 carry portraits of Alexius receiving scrolls from nine church fathers, and presenting the work to Christ.

91   For a clear methodological statement see Ellen Muehlberger, *Angels in Late Ancient Christianity* (Oxford: Oxford University Press, 2013), at 17–22, on "The religious imagination," referring also to the task of "parsing a culture."

92   Pierre Bourdieu, *Outline of a Theory of Practice* (Cambridge: Cambridge University Press, 1977); id., *Language and Symbolic Power* (Cambridge: Polity Press, 1991); id., *The Field of Cultural Production* (Cambridge: Polity Press, 1993).

93   Dan Chitoiu, "Ideology and Philosophy in Byzantium: The Meanings of Ideology before Modern Times," *Journal for the Study of Religions and Ideologies* 8.23 (2009), 48–67.

94   Pierre Bourdieu, *Distinction: A Social Critique of the Judgement of Taste* (London: Routledge, 1984); id., *Homo Academicus* (Cambridge: Polity Press, 1988).

95   Angold, *Church and Society*, chap. 1, 15–41, is entitled "Conflict and Debate," but refers to Byzantine "fossilization," 18.

Chapter 2

1   John F. Haldon, "The Byzantine Successor State." in *The Oxford Handbook of the State in the Ancient Near East and Mediterranean*, ed. Peter Fibiger Bang and Walter Scheidel (Oxford: Oxford University Press, 2013), 495.

2   Garth Fowden, *Before and After Muhammad: The First Millenium Refocused* (Princeton: Princeton University Press, 2014).

3   Fowden, *Before and After Muhammad*, 137–38, 149, 151.

4   Though see John F. Haldon, "The Byzantine Empire," in *The Dynamics of Ancient Empires*, ed. Ian Morris and Walter Scheidel, 224–73 (Oxford: Oxford University Press, 2008); moreover, two chapters in Peter Fibiger Bang and Dariusz Kołodziejczyk, eds., *Universal Empire: A Comparative Approach to Imperial Culture and Representation in Eurasian History* (Cambridge: Cambridge University Press, 2012), deal with Byzantine universalism.

5   As exemplified for instance in Jonathan Harris, Catherine Holmes and Eugenia Russell, eds., *Byzantines, Latins, and Turks in the Mediterranean World after 1150* (Oxford: Oxford University Press, 2012); see the introduction, 1–30, and Catherine Holmes, "Shared Worlds: Religious Identities – a Question of Evidence," ibid, 31–60, for a sensitive discussion of shared and fluid religious identities and the difficulties of interpreting certain sorts of evidence.

6   Or indeed vice versa: see Nilsson, *Raconter Byzance,* 214–20.

7   Magdalino, *Empire of Manuel I*, 407–408.

8   See Alex Novikoff, *The Medieval Culture of Disputation. Pedagogy, Practice and Performance* (Philadelphia: University of Pennsylvania Press, 2013), and for the comparison, Steckel, Gaul and Grünbart, eds., *Networks of Learning*; on the period R. I. Moore, *The First European Revolution, c. 970–1215* (Oxford: Blackwell, 2000).

9   Novikoff, *Medieval Culture*, 66; Latin translations of Aristotle's logical works: ibid., 106–18.

10   Ibid., 25–29.

11   Ibid., 67.

12   Tia M. Kolbaba, "The Orthodoxy of the Latins in the Twelfth Century," in *Byzantine Orthodoxies*, ed. Andrew Louth and Augustine Casiday, Society for the Promotion of Byzantine Studies Publications 12 (Aldershot: Ashgate, 2006), 199–214, discusses these issues for the twelfth century.

13   The concept of a "persecuting society" in relation to the medieval west was originally set out in 1987 by R. I. Moore; see id., *The Formation*

170

of a Persecuting Society: Power and Deviance in Western Europe, 950–1250, 2nd ed. (Oxford: Blackwell, 2007). Byzantium is absent from id., *The War on Heresy: Faith and Power in Medieval Europe* (London: Profile, 2014), but the history of heresiological literature in late antiquity and Byzantium is very long: see Averil Cameron, "How to Read Heresiology," *Journal of Medieval and Early Modern Studies* 33.3 (Fall, 2003): 471–92, also in, *The Cultural Turn in Late Ancient Studies: Gender, Asceticism and Historiography*, ed. Dale B. Martin and Patricia Cox Miller (Durham, NC: Duke University Press, 2005), 193–212.

14 Magdalino, *Empire of Manuel I*, 383: "Did Byzantium under the Komnenoi become even more of a persecuting society than it had been before?" At 393 Magdalino notes that Byzantium did not persecute as much as the west, but compare the term "persecuting mentality" at 388.

15 See Evelyne Patlagean, *Un Moyen Âge grec. Byzance, IXe–XVe siècle* (Paris: Albin Michel, 2007).

16 Macrides and Magdalino, "The Fourth Kingdom"; Kolbaba, "Byzantine Perceptions," 121–28, 134–40, shows that Byzantine perceptions of the Latins in the eleventh and twelfth centuries were more complex than they might seem.

17 *Alexiad* XV.9–10.

18 *PG* 130,19-1362. Reception: Nadia Miladinova, *The* Panoplia Dogmatike *by Euthymios Zygadenos: A Study on the First Edition Published in Greek in 1710* (Leiden: Brill, 2014); I thank Nadia Miladinova for giving me advance notice of her book.

19 For Soterichos see also Janet Hamilton, Sarah Hamilton and Bernard Hamilton, *Hugh Eteriano: Contra Patarenos* (Leiden: Brill, 2004), 114–15; Angold, *Church and Society*, 81–83.

20 A. Cataldi Palau, "*L'Arsenale Sacro* di Andronico Camatero, il proemi ed il dialogo dell'imperatore con i cardinali latini: originale, imitazioni, arrangiamenti," *REB* 51 (1993): 5–62; Bucossi, *Andronici Camateri*. For the *Filioque* see A. Edward Siecinski, *The Filioque: History of a Doctrinal Controversy* (Oxford: Oxford University Press, 2010).

21 *Sacred Arsenal*, § 74.

171

22   See Tia M. Kolbaba, *The Byzantine Lists: Errors of the Latins* (Urbana, Ill.: University of Illinois Press, 2000), 32–71.

23   For Andronikos Kamateros see Alessandra Bucossi, "The *Sacred Arsenal* by Andronikos Kamateros: A Forgotten Treasure," in Rigo and Ermilov, eds., *Byzantine Theologians*, 36–37; for Niketas Choniates see Alicia Simpson, *Niketas Choniates* (Oxford: Oxford University Press, 2013).

24   Simpson, *Niketas Choniates*, 36–44; Bossina, "Niketas Choniates," 179–83; and see chapter three. Bossina argues for the *Panoply* to be taken seriously rather than written off as derivative.

25   Bossina, "Niketas Choniates," 173–74; Zorzi, "Islam e Cristianesimo," 294.

26   For the practice see Rigo and Ermilov, *Byzantine Theologians*; for the citations and syllogisms in the *Sacred Arsenal* see Alessandra Bucossi, "Dialogues and Anthologies of the *Sacred Arsenal* by Andronikos Kamateros: Sources, Arrangements, Purposes," in *Encyclopaedic Trends in Byzantium*, ed. Peter Van Deun and Caroline Macé, Orientalia Lovaniensia Analecta 212 (Peeters: Leuven, 2011), 269–86.

27   Hans-Georg Beck, *Kirche und theologische Literatur im byzantinischen Reich* (Munich: C.H. Beck'sche Verlagsbuchhandlung, 1959), 618.

28   Bucossi, "Forgotten Treasure," 35.

29   Alexander Alexakis, *Codex Parisinus Graecus 1115 and its Archetype* (Washington, DC: Dumbarton Oaks, 1996).

30   Jean Darrouzès, *Documents inédits d'ecclesiologie byzantine* (Paris: Institut français d'études byzantines, 1966), 66–74, 310–31.

31   Börje Bydén, "'Strangle them with the Meshes of Syllogisms!': Latin Philosophy in Greek Translations of the Thirteenth Century," in *Interaction and Isolation in Late Byzantine Culture: Papers read at a colloquium held at the Swedish Research Institute in Istanbul, 1–5 December, 1999,* ed. Jan Olof Rosenqvist,Transactions of the Swedish Research Institute in Istanbul 13 (Stockholm: Swedish Research Institute in Istanbul, 2004), 133–57, explores some of the implications; as we saw, his liking for syllogisms formed part of the accusation against Eustratius of Nicaea in 1117.

32   The text can be found in Dositheos, *Tomos,* 527–38.

33 *PG* 139.169; on Niketas (of whose dialogues there is no complete critical edition), see Bucossi, "Dialogues and Anthologies." 279–83, and
    ead., "The Six Dialogues by Niketas 'of Maroneia': An Introduction,"
    forthcoming in Cameron and Gaul, eds., *Dialogues and Debates*, arguing for an earlier date than usually assigned to him.

34 On Hugo, see Hamilton, Hamilton and Hamilton, *Hugh Eteriano*,
    109–53; Antoine Dondaine, "Hugues Ethérien et le concile de Constantinople de 1166," *Hist. Jahrbuch* 77 (1958): 473–83.

35 Translation in Hamilton, Hamilton and Hamilton, *Hugh Eteriano*,
    132–34; text in Antoine Dondaine, "Hugues Éthérien et Léon Toscan." *Archives de l'histoire doctrinales et littéraires du Moyen Âge* 19
    (1952): 473–83.

36 Hamilton, Hamilton and Hamilton, *Hugh Eteriano*, 117–21.

37 *PL* 202. 227–396.

38 Hamilton, Hamilton and Hamilton, *Hugh Eteriano*, 138–39, 143–47.

39 Ibid., *Introduction*; on Latins in Constantinople, 11–12; on Cathars,
    99.

40 Kolbaba, "The Orthodoxy of the Latins," 214.

41 Bucossi, "Dialogues and Anthologies," 284.

42 Bucossi, "Dialogues and Anthologies." 279–80.

43 Bucossi, "Dialogues and Anthologies." 281.

44 Talal Asad, *Genealogies of Religion: Discipline and Reasons of Power in
    Christianity and Islam* (Baltimore: Johns Hopkins University Press,
    1993), 210, 236.

45 Eadmer, *Life of Anselm,* 112–13, cited by Novikoff, *Medieval Culture*, 97; on Anselm of Havelberg see Novikoff, ibid., 95–100, with
    Novikoff, "Anselm of Havelberg's Controversies with the Greeks:
    A Moment in the Scholastic Culture of Disputation," in Cameron and
    Gaul, eds., *Dialogues and Debates*.

46 For the first English translation of Anselm's *Anticeimenon*, see Ambrose Criste and Carol Need, *Anselm of Havelberg, Anticimenon: On
    the Unity of Faith and the Controversies with the Greeks*, Cistercian
    Studies 232 (Collegeville, Minn.: Liturgical Press, 2010); see Kolbaba, "The Orthodoxy of the Latins." 212.

47 *PL* 188. 1139.

173

48 Angold, *Church and Society*, 92–93; Magdalino, *Empire of Manuel I*, 325–27.

49 See on this Novikoff, *Medieval Culture*.

50 See Jay T. Lees, *Anselm of Havelberg: Deeds into Words in the Twelfth Century* (Leiden: Brill, 1998); Norman Russell, "Anselm of Havelberg and the Union of the Churches," *Sobornorst* 1 (1979): 19–41; J. Spiteris is unusual in addressing the Byzantine side, but still mainly focuses on Anselm: "Attitudes fondamentales de la théologie byzantine, en face du role de la papauté au XIIème siècle," in *The Religious Roles of the Papacy*, ed. Christopher Ryan (Toronto, 1989), 171–92. Siecienski, *The Filioque*, 121–24, gives a brief but somewhat more balanced account, though not addressing the issues of composition or dialogue technique.

51 Karl F. Morrison, "Anselm of Havelberg: Play and the Dilemma of Historical Progress," in Thomas X. Noble and John J. Contreni, eds.,*Religion, Culture and Society in the Early Middle Ages: Studies in Honor of Richard E. Sullivan* (Kalamazoo, 1987), 240; Morrison admits that the text is a "recasting," not a transcript, and "a work of rhetorical, or poetic, invention" (238, 220).

52 Walter H. Principe, "Monastic, Episcopal and Apologetic Theology of the Papacy, 1150–1250," in Ryan, ed., *The Religious Roles of the Papacy*, 132.

53 Lees, *Anselm of Havelberg*, 235–37.

54 *PL* 188.1187.

55 Paul Zumthor, *La lettre et la voix: De la "littérature" médiévale* (Paris: Éditions du Seuil, 1987), 92, cited by Lees, *Anselm of Havelberg*, 234.

56 Ibid., 237.

57 *PG* 119.927C, 929C.

58 I owe these points to Foteini Spingou.

59 J. Schmidt, *Des Basilius aus Achrida, Erzbischofs von Thessalonich bisher unedierte Dialoge. Ein Beitrag zur Geschichte des griechischen Schismas* (Munich, 1901); I owe this point also to Foteini Spingou.

60 Magdalino, *Empire of Manuel I*, 367, n. 174.

61 It is difficult to be precise about the identification of Bogomils as the source of the Cathar heresy; see Yuri Stoyanov, *The Other God: Dualist*

Religions from Antiquity to the Cathar Heresy (New Haven: Yale University Press, 2000), with Dimitri Obolensky, *The Bogomils: A Study in Balkan Neo-Manichaeism* (Cambridge: Cambridge University Press, 1948).

62   The importance of naming: Pierre Bourdieu, *Language and Symbolic Power* (Cambridge: Polity Press, 1991), 236.

63   For the Latins presented as heretics, see Kolbaba, *The Byzantine Lists*, and see her *Inventing Latin Heretics: Byzantines and the Filioque in the Ninth Century* (Western Michigan: Medieval Institute Publications, 2008); for assimilation to Jews, Kolbaba, "Byzantines, Armenians, Latins," 55–56.

64   For the phenomenon, Demacopoulos and Papanikolaou, eds., *Orthodox Constructions of the West.*

65   George E. Demacopoulos and Aristotle Papanikolauou, "Orthodox Naming of the Other: A Post-Colonialist Approach," in Demacopoulos and Papanikolaou, *Orthodox Constructions of the West*, 1–22; see also Evelyne Patlagean,"Byzance dans le millénaire médiéval," *Annales Histoire Sciences Sociales* 60.4 (2005): 721–29.

66   Kolbaba sees a development in Byzantine argument against the Latins between 1112 and 1136 ("The Orthodoxy of the Latins," 213).

67   *PL* 127, 911–19.

68   Text in Demetrakopoulos, *Ekklesiastike Bibliotheke*, 36–47.

69   Niketas Seides: Kolbaba, "Byzantine Perceptions," 126; see Bucossi, "The Six Dialogues by Niketas 'of Maroneia.'"

70   For this much debated change see Macrides and Magdalino, "The Fourth Kingdom"; Roderick Beaton, "Antique Nation?: 'Hellenes' on the Eve of Independence and in Twelfth-Century Byzantium," *BMGS* 31.1 (2007): 76–85.

71   The wide variation in the uses of the term is clear from Katerina Zacharia, ed., *Hellenisms: Culture, Identity and Ethnicity from Antiquity to Modernity* (Aldershot: Ashgate, 2008). Kaldellis, *Hellenism*, presents Byzantium as "the nation-state of the Romans"; but see 295–99 on "anti-Latin Hellenism," stronger after 1204; on Kaldellis's arguments see Ioannis Stauraitis, "Roman Identity in Byzantium: A Critical Approach," *BZ* 107.1 (2014): 199–200; Hellenism: 202–20 (for the term

"Graikos" see 208). Niketas Siniossoglou, *Radical Platonism in Byzantium: Illumination and Utopia in Gemistos Plethon* (Cambridge: Cambridge University Press, 2011), argues for an essentialist Hellenism persisting in opposition to Orthodox Christianity throughout the history of Byzantium.

72 Papaioannou, *Michael Psellos*, 169, 191.

73 Wider discussion of identity: Peter J. Burke and Jan E. Stets, *Identity Theory* (New York: Oxford University Press, 2009).

74 See Tia M. Kolbaba, "Byzantine Perceptions." 141–43. A bibliography on "identity" in relation to Byzantium running to seven pages can be found at http://byzideo.blogspot.co.at (accessed 20.9.15) while a conference on "Identity, Ethnicity and Nationhood before Modernity" held recently in Oxford attracted nearly one hundred papers over three days.

75 Macrides and Magdalino, "The Fourth Kingdom," 156; see also Kolbaba, "Byzantines, Armenians, Latins."

76 Dialogue and argument for a thirteenth-century date: Vitalien Laurent and Jean Darrouzès, *Dossier grec de l'Union de Lyon (1273–1277)* (Paris: Archives de l'Orient Chrétien, 1976), 45–52, 346–75; see Magdalino, *Empire of Manuel I*, 292–93.

77 See Christopher MacEvitt, *The Crusades and the Christian World of the East: Rough Tolerance* (Philadelphia: University of Pennsylvania Press, 2008), 157–79; Nerses IV and Theorianos: 165–67.

78 Ed. Demetrakopoulos, *Ekklesiastike*, 160–98.

79 *PG* 133.122-212, 232-98, preceded by an exchange of official letters. See Bucossi, "New Historical Evidence," 126–27.The extensive correspondence between the Armenians and Constantinople, though not the *Dialexeis*, has been recently translated and discussed by Isabelle Augé, *Églises en dialogue: Arméniens et Byzantins dans la seconde moitié du XIIe siècle*, CSCO 633, Subsidia 124 (Louvain: Peeters, 2011).

80 See Paul Magdalino, "Prosopography and Byzantine Identity," in Averil Cameron, ed., *Fifty Years of Byzantine Prosopography: The Later Roman Empire, Byzantium and Beyond* (Oxford: Oxford University Press for the British Academy, 2003), 53–54.

81 Linda Safran, *The Medieval Salento. Art and Identity in Southern Italy* (Philadelphia: University of Pennsylvania Press, 2014), 214.

176

82 Andrew Stone, "Nerses IV 'the Gracious', Manuel I Komnenos, the Patriarch Michael III Anchialos and Negotiations for Church Union between Byzantium and the Armenian Church, 1165–73," *JÖB* 55 (2005): 181–208.

83 Augé, *Églises en dialogue*, 68.

84 *PG* 133.165.

85 See also Isabelle Augé, *Byzantins, Arméniens et Francs au temps de la croisade. Politique religieuse et reconquête en Orient sous la dynastie des Comnènes, 1081–1185* (Paris: S.N. Librairie Orientale Paul Geuthner, 2007); Abraham Teriyan, "To Byzantium with Love: The Overtures of Saint Nerses the Gracious," in *Armenian Cilicia*, ed. Richard G. Hovannisian and Simon Payaslian (Costa Mesa, CA: Mazda Publishers Inc., 2008), 131–57.

86 *PG* 133.124; 233.

87 *PG* 133. 233–36, 224–32.

88 Augé, *Églises en dialogue*, 300–301.

89 Above, n. 77.

Chapter 3

1 Rita George-Tvrtković, *A Christian Pilgrim in Medieval Iraq: Riccoldo da Monte Croce's Encounter with Islam* (Turnhout: Brepols, 2012); Riccoldo wrote in the aftermath of the fall of Acre in 1291.

2 Natalie Zemon Davis, *Trickster Travels: A Sixteenth-Century Muslim between Worlds* (New York: Hill and Wang, 2006).

3 Indeed John Tolan's introduction to his book *Saracens: Islam in the Medieval European Imagination* (New York: Columbia University Press, 2002), xiii–xxiii, is entitled "Riccoldo's Predicament, or, How to Explain Away the Successes of a Flourishing Rival Civilization."

4 For this well-known Hebrew text see M. N. Adler, *The Itinerary of Benjamin of Tudela: Critical Edition, Translation and Commentary* (London, 1907), and see David Jacoby, "Benjamin of Tudela in Byzantium," *Palaeoslavica* 10 (2002), 180–85; David Jacoby, "Benjamin of Tudela and his Book of Travels," in *Venezia, incrocio di culture*, ed.

Klaus Herbers and Felicitas Schmieder (Rome: Edizioni di storia e letteratura, 2008), 1000–1030.

5   The plausibility of these numbers is of course impossible to check: for a useful discussion see Béatrice Caseau, *Byzance: économie et société. Du milieu du VIIIe siècle à 1204* (Paris: Sedes, 2007), 292–98.

6   Nicholas de Lange, "Jewish Education in the Byzantine Empire in the Twelfth Century," in *Jewish Education and Learning*, ed. Glenda Abramson and Tudor Parfitt, (London: Harwood Academic Publishers, 1994), 115–28, at 116–18; de Lange gives a list of Jewish scholars and writers in Constantinople, ibid, 122; for the evidence from the Genizah see de Lange, "Byzantium in the Cairo Genizah," *BMGS* 16 (1992): 34–47. I am very grateful to Nicholas de Lange for his comments and suggestions on an earlier draft of this chapter.

7   This fence or wall was erected at the end of the eleventh century after a fierce quarrel between the two groups over the date of the Jewish Passover, when the Byzantine authorities had to intervene: see David Jacoby, "The Jewish Community in Constantinople from the Komnenan to the Palaiologan Period," *Vizantiijski Vremennik* 55 (1998): 31–40, repr. in id., *Byzantium, Latin Romania and the Mediterranean* (Aldershot: Ashgate, 2001), no.V, at 32–33.

8   See for instance de Lange, "Hebrew Scholarship in Byzantium"; the same sparsity applies to Hebrew inscriptions in the Byzantine period: Nicholas de Lange, "Hebrew Inscriptions of the Byzantine Empire," in *Manuscrits hébreux et arabes. Mélanges en l'honneur de Colette Sirat*, ed. Nicholas de Lange and Judith Olszowy-Schlanger, Bibliologia 38 (Turnhout: Brepols, 2014), 415–24.

9   Samuel Krauss and William Horbury, *The Jewish-Christian Controversy from the Earliest Times to 1789,* I, *History* (Tübingen: Mohr Siebeck, 1996), 61–68.

10   Patrick Andrist, "The Greek Bible used by the Jews in the dialogues *Contra Iudaeos* (fourth-tenth centuries CE)," in *Jewish Receptions of Greek Bible Versions: Studies in their Use in Late Antiquity and the Middle Ages*, ed. Nicholas de Lange, Julia G. Krivoruchko and Cameron Boyd-Taylor (Tübingen: Mohr Siebeck, 2009), 235–61.

11   The recent volume edited by Robert Bonfil, Oded Irshai, Gedaliu G.

Stroumsa, and Rina Talgam, *Jews in Byzantium: Dialectics of Minority and Majority Cultures* (Leiden: Brill, 2012) is also particularly welcome.

12 I am indebted here to Nicholas de Lange's 2015 Grinfield Lectures on the Septuagint, not yet published.

13 Robert Bonfil, "Continuity and Discontinuity (641–1204)," in *Jews in Byzantium*, ed. Bonfil, Irshai, Stroumsa and Talgam, 76–100.

14 On Heraclius: Paul Magdalino, " 'All Israel will be Saved'?: The Forced Baptism of Jews and Imperial Eschatology," in *Jews in Early Christian Law: Byzantium and the West, 6ᵗʰ to 11ᵗʰ Centuries*, ed. John Tolan, Nicholas de Lange, Laurence Foschia and Capucine Nemo-Pekelman (Turnhout: Brepols, 2013), 231–42; Basil I: Oscar Prieto Domínguez, "The Mass Conversion of Jews Decreed by Emperor Basil I in 873–74: Its Reflection in Contemporary Legal Codes and its Underlying Reasons," ibid, 283–310, attributing a key role to the patriarch Photius.

15 Gilbert Dagron, "Le traité de Grégoire de Nicée sur le baptême des Juifs," *Travaux et Mémoires* 11 (1991): 313–57.

16 Bonfil, "Continuity and Discontinuity," 97; on the conversion of the Jews as a key hagiographical theme see Youval Rotman, "Converts in Byzantine Italy: Local Representations of Jewish-Christian Rivalry," in Bonfil, Irshai, Stroumsa, Targam, eds., *Jews in Byzantium*, 904–8.

17 See Immacolata Aulisa, *Guidei e cristiani nell'agiografia dell'alto Medioevo* (Bari: Edipuglia, 2009); ead., "La polemica *adversus Iudaeos* nell'agiografia dell'alto medioevo," in *Les dialogues* Adversus Iudaeos. *Permanences et mutations d'une tradition polémique*, ed. Sébastien Morlet, Olivier Munnich, Bernard Pouderon, *Actes du colloque international organisé les 7. et 8. décembre 2011 à l'Université de Paris-Sorbonne* (Paris: Institut d'Études Augustiniennes, 2013), 269–94; also Vera von Falkenhausen, "In Search of the Jews in Byzantine Literature," in Bonfil, Irshai, Stroumsa, Targam, eds., *Jews in Byzantium*, 871–91.

18 Rotman, "Converts in Byzantine Italy," 919.

19 See Dominique Iogna-Prat, *Order and Exclusion: Cluny and Christendom Face Heresy, Judaism and Islam (1000–1150)* (Ithaca, NY: Cornell University Press, 2002), 276, with 275–322 on Peter's anti-Jewish writing; see also Robert Chazan, "Twelfth-Century Perceptions of the Jews: A Case Study of Bernard of Clairvaux and Peter the Ven-

erable," in *From Witness to Witchcraft: Jews and Judaism in Medieval Christian Thought*, ed. Jeremy Cohen,Wolfenbütteler Mittelalter-Studien 11 (Wiesbaden: Harassowitz Verlag, 1996), 187–201.

20 David Jacoby, "Les quartiers juifs de Constantinople à l'époque byzantine," *Byzantion* 37 (1967): 167–227 (reprinted in Jacoby, *Société et démographie à Byzance et en Romanie latine* (London: Variorum, 1975), no. II); Jacoby, "The Jews of Constantinople and their Demographic Hinterland," in *Constantinople and its Hinterland*, ed. Cyril Mango and Gilbert Dagron (Aldershot: Variorum, 1995), 221–32 (reprinted in Jacoby, *Byzantium, Latin Romania and the Mediterranean*, no. IV [Aldershot: Ashgate, 2001]), at 222–23; immigration into Constantinople: ibid., 223–28; see also Jacoby, "The Jewish Community in Constantinople." Map, sources and bibliography of the Jewish quarters in Constantinople and elsewhere in the empire are available at Nicholas de Lange, Alexander Panayotov and Gethin Rees, *Mapping the Jewish Communities of the Byzantine Empire* (2013), at www.byzantinejewry.net (accessed 20.9.15).

21 On the developments in this area and the arrival of the Italians see Paul Magdalino, *Constantinople médiévale. Études sur l'évolution des structure urbaines* (Paris: De Boccard, 1996), 78–80.

22 Krauss and Horbury, *The Jewish-Christian Controversy* I, 64, 67; see also Daniel J. Lasker, "Jewish-Christian Polemics at the Turning-Point: Jewish Evidence from the Twelfth Century," *HThR* 89.2 (1996): 161–73.

23 Judah Hadassi: Krauss and Horbury, *The Jewish-Christian Controversy* I, 218; Golda Akhiezer, "Byzantine Karaism in the Eleventh to Fifteenth Centuries," in Bonfil, Irshai, Stroumsa and Talgam, eds., *Jews in Byzantium*, 728–33.

24 Jewish apologetics: William Horbury, "Hebrew Apologetic and Polemical Literature," in de Lange, ed., *Hebrew Scholarship and the Medieval World*, 189–209, especially 196–99; Jeremy Cohen, "Towards a Functional Classification of Jewish Anti-Christian Polemic in the High Middle Ages," in *Religionsgespräche im Mittelalter*, ed. Bernard Lewis and Friedrich Niewöhner (Wiesbaden: Harassowitz, 1992), 93–114; see also Nicholas de Lange, "A Fragment of Byzantine Anti-

Christian Polemic," *JJS* 41 (1990): 92–100, for a fragment of a polemical treatise, seemingly from around the twelfth century, written in a mixture of Hebrew and Greek.

25 Justin, *Dialogue with Trypho*: Cameron, *Dialoguing in Late Antiquity*, 15, 17; overviews of the *Adversus Iudaeos* literature: Heinz Schreckenberg, *Die christlichen Adversus Iudaeos Texte (11.–13.Jh.)*, 4 ed. (Frankfurt am Main: Peter Lang, 1999); Andreas Külzer, *Disputationes Graecae contra Iudaeos. Untersuchungen zur byzantinischen antijüdischen Dialogliteratur und ihrem Judenbild*, Byzantinisches Archiv 18 (Berlin: De Gruyter, 1999), with discussion of dialogues at 74–88, and Byzantine *Adversus Iudaeos* texts at 88–92.

26 For these see Sidney H. Griffith, *The Church in the Shadow of the Mosque: Christians and Muslims in the World of Islam* (Princeton, NJ: Princeton University Press, 2008), and *Christian-Muslim Relations: A Bibliographical History*, ed. David Thomas et al., 7 vols. (Leiden: Brill, 2009), of which vol. 3 (2011) deals with the period 1050–1200.

27 Patrick Andrist, "The Physiognomy of Greek *Contra Iudaeos* Manuscript Books in the Byzantine Era: A Preliminary Survey," in Bonfil, Irshai, Stroumsa and Targam, eds., *Jews in Byzantium*, 562–72.

28 For an overview see Bernhard Blumenkranz, *Les auteurs chrétiens latins du moyen âge sur les juifs et le judaïsme*, 2ⁿᵈ ed. (Paris-Louvain: Peeters, 2007).

29 Novikoff, *Medieval Culture*, 52–55.

30 Krauss and Horbury, *The Jewish-Christian Controversy* I, 72–78, 101–102.

31 The Jewish communities of south Italy were described in the *Chronicle of Ahimaaz*, by a Jew from Capua in 1054: see Youval Rotman, "Christians, Jews and Muslims in Southern Italy: Medieval Conflicts in Local Perspective," in Stephenson, ed., *The Byzantine World*, 231; Rotman, "Converts in Byzantine Italy," 912–14.

32 M. Chrontz, ed., Νεκταρίου, ἡγουμένου μονῆς Κασούλων Νικολάου Ὑδρουντινοῦ, Διάλεξις κατὰ Ιουδαίων (Athens, 2009); discussion in Johannes M. Hoeck and Raimund J. Loenertz, *Nikolaos-Nektarios von Otranto, Abt von Casole. Beiträge zur Geschichte der ost-westlichen Beziehungen unter Innocent III und Friedrich II* (Ettal: Buch-Kunst-

verlag Ettal, 1965); see also Claudio Schiano, "Il *Dialogo contro I gui-dei* di Nicola di Otranto tra fonti storiche e teologiche," in Morlet, Munnich, Pouderon, eds., *Les dialogues* Adversus Iudaeos, 295–317.

33 See the rich material on Jews in south Italy in Vera von Falkenhausen, "The Jews in Byzantine Southern Italy," in Bonfil, Irshai, Stroumsa and Talgam, eds., *Jews in Byzantium*, 271–96; for Otranto, with mention of Nicolas as "one of its great intellectuals," see 288–90. Nicolas also wrote anti-Latin works: Safran, *The Medieval Salento*, 213 (and see her remarks on the complexities of religious identity and the interplay of language in south Italy).

34 So Steven Bowman, *The Jews of Byzantium, 1204–1453* (Atlanta: University of Alabama Press, 1985), 33.

35 Schiano, "Il *Dialogo contro I guidei*," 308–11.

36 The same Nicolas and his group of followers also produced religious and secular poems, epigrams and treatises: Linda Safran, "A Medieval Ekphrasis from Otranto," *BZ* 83 (1990): 425–27.

37 Jacoby, "The Jews of Constantinople," 37–38.

38 Schiano, "Il *Dialogo contro I guidei*," 299–302; Karaites in Byzantium: Akhiezer, "Byzantine Karaism."

39 Evelyne Patlagean, "La 'Dispute avec les Juifs' de Nicolas d'Otrante (vers 1220) et la question du Messie," in *La storia degli Ebrei nell'Italia meridionale: tra filologia e metodologia*, ed. M. G. Muzzarelli and G. Todeschini (Bologna: Istituto per i beni artistici, culturali e naturali della Regione Emilia-Romagna, 1990), 19–27; see Arsenio Frugoni, Adversus Iudaeos *di Gioacchino da Fiore* (Rome: Nella sede dell'Istituto, 1957).

40 Schiano, "Il *Dialogo contro I guidei*," 302.

41 Ibid., 311–16.

42 Antonio Rigo, "Messalianismo=Bogomilismo. Un equazione dell'eresiologia medievale bizantina," *OCP* 56 (1990): 53–82.

43 Schiano, "Il *Dialogo contro I guidei,*'" 314–16.

44 In general for these works see Anna Sapir Abulafia, "The Service of Jews in Christian-Jewish Disputations," in Morlet, Munnich and Pouderon, eds., *Les dialogues* Adversus Iudaeos, 339–50; Anna Sapir Abulafia, *Christians and Jews in the Twelfth-Century Renaissance* (Lon-

don: Routledge, 1995); Anna Sapir Abulafia, *Christians and Jews in Dispute: Disputational Literature and the Rise of Anti-Judaism in the West (c. 1000–1150)* (Aldershot: Variorum. 1998); Anna Sapir Abulafia, *Christian-Jewish Relations, 1000–1300: Jews in the Service of Medieval Christendom* (New York: Pearson Education Ltd, 2011). Peter Alfonsi also digresses from his main topic in order to denounce Islam: Novikoff, *Medieval Culture*, 180, n.44. For an illustration of this imaginary debate between Peter's two personae from a thirteenth-century manuscript see Novikoff, *Medieval Culture*, 183, fig. 10.

45   For discussion of these issues in relation to Herman the Jew see Jean-Claude Schmitt, *La conversion d'Herman le juif: autobiographie, histoire et fiction* (Paris: Éditions du Seuil, 2003); for dialogues see 155–61, "De Gilbert Crispin à Pierre Alphonse."

46   Deborah L. Goodwin, "'Nothing in *our* Histories': A Post-Colonial Perspective on Twelfth-Century Christian Hebraism," *Medieval Encounters* 15 (2009): 35–65, especially 43–47; see also 62.

47   Hartwig Hirschfeld, *Judah Hallevi's* Kitab al Khazari, rev. ed. (London: M. L. Callingold, 1931); Joseph Yahalom, "The Journey Inward: Judah Halevi between Christians and Muslims in Spain, Egypt and Palestine," in de Lange, ed., *Hebrew Scholarship and the Medieval World*, 138–48.

48   Schreckenberg, *Die christlichen Adversus Iudaeos Texte (11.–13.Jh.)*, 133–44; Novikoff, *Medieval Culture*, 184–85.

49   Novikoff, *Medieval Culture*, 176–78 (Anselm of Canterbury and Gilbert Crispin), 182 (Peter Alfonsi); cf. 182 on the utility of "the hermeneutic Jew" (below); see also the works by Sapir Abulafia already mentioned, with Blumenkranz, *Les auteurs chrétiens latins*; Gilbert Dahan, *The Christian Polemic against Jews in the Middle Ages* (Notre Dame: University of Notre Dame Press, 1998); Gilbert Dahan, "Les questions d'exégèse dans les dialogues contre les juifs XIIe-XIIIe siècles," in Morlet, Munnich and Pouderon, eds., *Les dialogues* Adversus Iudaeos, 319–37.

50   For a Syriac example probably from the early Islamic period see Adam H. Becker, "The Discourse of Priesthood (BL Add. 18295, ff. 137b–140b): An Anti-Jewish Text on the Abrogation of the Israelite Priesthood," *JSS* 51.1 (2006), 85–115.

183

51 See David Berger, "Mission to the Jews and Christian-Jewish Contacts in the Polemical Literature of the High Middle Ages," *AHR* 91 (1986): 576–91; Gavin I. Langmuir, "Mission to the Jews and Jewish-Christian Contexts: Scholarship and Intolerance in the Medieval Academy: Comment," *AHR* 91 (1986): 614–24; Jeremy Cohen, ed., *Essential Papers on Judaism and Christianity in Conflict, from Late Antiquity to the Reformation* (New York: New York University Press, 1991).

52 Bonfil, "Continuity and Discontinuity," 94; despite the promise of its title this article does not discuss the twelfth century in detail.

53 Steven Bowman, "Twelfth-Century Jewish Responses to Crusade and *jihad,*" in *Crusaders, Condottieri and Cannon: Medieval Warfare in Societies around the Mediterranean,* ed. Donald J. Kagay and L. J. Andrew Villalon (Leiden: Brill, 2003), 417–38.

54 Tolan, *Saracens,* 135–69.

55 Stephen F. Kruger, "Medieval Christian (Dis)identifications: Muslims and Jews in Guibert of Nogent," *New Literary History* 28.2 (997): 185–203.

56 Thomas E. Burman, *Reading the Qur'an in Latin Christendom, 1140–1560.* Philadelphia: University of Pennsylvania Press, 2007.

57 For a survey see David R. Blanks, "Western Views of Islam in the Premodern Period: A Brief History of Past Approaches," in Frassetto and Blanks, eds., *Western Views of Islam,* 11–53.

58 For instance in the survey by John Meyendorff, "Byzantine Views of Islam," *DOP* 18 (1964): 115–32.

59 For an introduction to these texts see Averil Cameron and Robert Hoyland, eds., *Doctrine and Debate in the East Christian World, 300–1500* (Farnham: Ashgate, 2011), xxx–xxxiii, and see Wolfgang Eichner, "Byzantine Accounts of Islam," in Cameron and Hoyland, *Doctrine and Debate,* 109–70; see also Robert Hoyland, *Seeing Islam as Others Saw It: A Survey and Evaluation of Christian, Jewish and Zoroastrian Writings on Early Islam,* Studies in Late Antiquity and Early Islam 13 (Princeton, NJ: the Darwin Press, Inc., 1997).

60 Chapter on Islam: Raymond Le Coz, *Jean Damascène. Écrits sur l'Islam,* Sources chrétiennes 383 (Paris: Cerf, 1992); *Dispute between a Saracen and a Christian*: CPG 8075, ed. Kotter, IV, 420–38; cf.

André-Louis Rey,"Remarques sur la forme et l'utilisation de passages dialogués entre chrétiens et musulmans dans le corpus de Saint Jean Damascène," in Anastasia Lazaridis, Vincent Barras, and Terpsichore Birchler, eds., *Boukoleia. Mélanges offerts à Bertrand Bouvier*, ed. (Geneva: Editions des Belles-Lettres, 1995), 69–83.

61 Hoyland, in Cameron and Hoyland, eds. *Doctrine and Debate,* xxxix; the point is also made by Sidney Griffith.

62 Erich Trapp, "Gab es eine byzantinische Koranübersetzung?," *Diptycha* 2 (1980–81): 7–17; Asterios Argyriou, "Perception de l'Islam et traductions du Coran dans le monde byzantin grec," *Byzantion* 75 (2005): 25–69; Antonio Rigo, '"Gli Ismaeliti e la discendenza da Abramo nella 'Refutazione del Corano' di Niceta Byzantios (meta del IX secolo)," in Giuseppe Ruggieri, ed., *I nemici dello cristianità*, (Bologna: Il Mulino, 1997), 83–104; Antonio Rigo, "Niceta Bizantios. La sua opera e il monaco Evodio," in *In partibus Clius. Scritti in onore di Giovanni Pugliese Carratelli*, ed. Gianfranco Fiaccadori, with Andrea Gatti and Sergio Marotta (Naples: Vivarium, 2006), 147–87.

63 *PG* 131.20–40; Erich Trapp, "Die *Dialexis* des Mönchs Euthymios mit einem Sarazenen," *JÖB* 20 (1971): 114–31.

64 Alain Ducellier, *Chrétiens d'Orient et l'Islam au Moyen Âge, VIIe – XVe siècle* (Paris: Armand Colin/Masson, 1996), 277–80. Another Greek example from the late twelfth or thirteenth century, though not from Constantinople, is the refutation of "an Agarene" by Bartholomew of Edessa, which starts with questions and answers and then turns into a treatise: Klaus-Peter Todt, *Bartholomaios von Edessa, Confutatio Agareni*, Corpus Islamo-Christianum,Series Graeca 2 (Würzburg and Altenberge: Echter Verlag-Telos Verlag, 1988).

65 Erich Trapp, ed., *Dialoge mit einem "Perser,"* Wiener byz. Stud. 2 (Vienna: In Kommission bei G. Böhlaus, Nachf, 1966).

66 Kydones's translation: *PG* 154.1035–1152, probably from 1154–60; Riccoldo's original Latin text does not survive.

67 Magdalino, *Empire of Manuel*, 297–98.

68 Zorzi, "Islam e Cristianesimo," 280–86, with bibliography, and see Andrew F. Stone, "The Missionaries of Manuel I," *REB 66* (2008): 253–57, at 255–57.

69 Magdalino, *Empire of Manuel I*, 95–98.

70 Ibid., 123–32; see 129–32 on the encomium on Niketas Choniates by his brother Michael, and the situation of Niketas's bishopric and birthplace of Chonai in Phrygia. In general, see Ducellier, *Chrétiens d'Orient et l'Islam*, especially 260–82; movements of population, also affecting religious issues and questions of conversion: Michel Balard and Alain Ducellier, *Migrations et Diasporas Méditerranéennes (Xe–XVIe siècles)* (Paris: Publications de la Sorbonne, 2002); the westward move of Armenians in the late tenth century presented just such issues, see Gilbert Dagron, "Minorités ethniques et religieuses dans l'orient byzantin à la fin du X et au XI siècle: l'immigration syrienne," *Travaux et Mémoires* 6 (1976): 177–216.

71 Simpson, *Niketas Choniates*, 45; Craig L. Hanson, "Manuel I Comnenus and the 'God of Muhammad': A Study in Byzantine Ecclesiastical Politics," in *Medieval Perceptions of Islam*, ed. John Tolan (London: Routledge, 1996), 65–71; according to Magdalino, *Empire of Manuel I*, 103–104, Manuel was motivated by the belief that Kiliç Arslan II wanted to marry his son to Frederick Barbarossa's daughter, and had reportedly asked the pope for instruction in Christianity, but for Manuel's interest in the conversion of Muslims see Zorzi, "Islam e Cristianesimo," 301–308. Dimitri Korobeinikov, "A Sultan In Constantinople: The Feasts of Ghiyāth al-Dīn Kay-Khusraw I," in *Eat, Drink and be Merry (Luke 12:19): Food and Wine in Byzantium*, ed. Leslie Brubaker and Kallirroe Linardou (Aldershot: Ashgate, 2007), 103, describes Manuel's diplomatic generosity to the sultan on his visit to Constantinople in 1161 (extending to the idea of a joint celebration in Hagia Sophia) and doubts the truth of the marriage story.

72 Zorzi, "Islam e Cristianesimo," 287–300; western views: John Tolan, "Saracen Philosophers Secretly Deride Islam," *Medieval Encounters* 8.2 (2002), 184–208; Tolan, *Saracens*, 105–34; Tolan "Muslims as Pagan Idolaters in Chronicles of the First Crusade," in *Western Views of Islam in Medieval and Early Modern Europe*, ed. Michael Frassetto and David R. Blanks (Basingstoke: Macmillan, 1999), 97–117.

73 See Paolo Eleuteri and Antonio Rigo, *Eretici, dissidenti, musulmani ed ebrei a Bisanzio: una raccolta eresiologica del XII secolo* (Venice: Il Cardo, 1993), with Edouard Montet, "Un ritual d'abjuration des Musul-

mans dans l'église grecque," *Rev. de l'histoire des religions* 53 (1906): 145–63; Hoyland, *Seeing Islam,* 517–18; Evelyne Patlagean, "Aveux et désaveux d'hérétiques à Byzance (XIe-XIIe siècles)," in *L'Aveu, antiquité et moyen-âge,* Actes de la table ronde organisée par l'Ecole française de Rome, avec le concours du CNRS et de l'Université de Trieste, Rome, 28–30 mars 1984 (Rome: École française de Rome, 1986), 243–60.

74 Abjuration formulae for Paulicians: Charles Astruc et al., "Les sources grecques pour l'histoire des Pauliciens d'Asie Mineure: texte critique et traduction," *Travaux et Mémoires* 4 (1970): 180–208, and for the twelfth century see also P. Ioannou, "Le sort des évêques hérétiques réconciliés: le discours inédit de Nicétas de Serres contre Eustrate de Nicée," *Byzantion* 28 (1958): 1–30.

75 Bonfil, "Continuity and Discontinuity," 94–95.

76 This and other examples: Rotman, "Converts in Byzantine Italy," 904–908; mass conversion as a late antique literary *topos*: ibid., 911; in Byzantine hagiography: von Falkenhausen, "In Search of the Jews," 879–82.

77 Barbara Crostini, "Christianity and Judaism in Eleventh-Century Constantinople," in Vincenzo Ruggieri and Luca Pieralli, eds., Eukosmia. Studi miscellanei per il 75° di Vincenzo Poggi S.J. (Soveria Mannelli, CZ: Rubbettino, 2003), 184. I am not sure that I follow Crostini in considering the tone of Byzantine representation of Jews in the eleventh century as gentle or conciliatory.

78 *PG* 154.372–692; Klaus-Peter Todt, *Kaiser Johannes VI Kantakuzenos und der Islam. Politische Realität und theologische Polemik im palaiologenzeitlichen Byzanz,* Würzburger Forschungen zur Missions- und Religionswissenschaft, Religionswissenschaftliche Studien 16 (Würzburg, 1991). John VI also wrote a work against the Jews cast as a discussion with "a Pharisee of the tribe of Judah called Xenos," whom he supposedly met in Mistra, who asks for baptism at the end of the debate.

79 Sapir Abulafia, "The Service of Jews"; Augustine: David Nirenberg, *Anti-Judaism: The History of a Way of Thinking* (London: Head of Zeus, 2013), 123–34, 269–99, with Paula Frederiksen, *Augustine and*

187

the Jews: A Christian Defense of Jews and Judaism, 2nd ed. with Post-script (New Haven: Yale University Press, 2010); Augustine in Byzantium: Barbara Crostini, "Augustine in the Byzantine World to 1453," in Karla Pollman, ed., *The Oxford Guide to the Reception of Augustine,* 3 vols (Oxford: Oxford University Press, 2013), II, 726–34; Josef Lössl, "Augustine in Byzantium," *JEH* 51 (2000): 267–95.

80 According to Rotman, "the Christian-Jewish conflict is presented as an entirely internal Byzantine religious affair," while "the Muslims, on the other hand, are portrayed as outsiders, and the Christian-Muslim relationship is portrayed as it was perceived at the time, as a political danger" (Rotman, "Christians, Jews and Muslims in Southern Italy," 230).

81 Zorzi, "Islam e Cristianesimo," 305–308.

82 Peter Frankopan, *The First Crusade: The Call from the East* (London: Bodley Head, 2012), 46–49.

83 Frankopan, *First Crusade,* 50–52; the recovery did not last and Antioch soon fell to the Turks.

84 For the mosques and for Muslims in Constantinople, Ducellier, *Chrétiens d'Orient et l'Islam,* 266; Glaire D. Anderson, "Islamic spaces and diplomacy in Constantinople (tenth to thirteenth centuries C.E.)," *Medieval Encounters* 15 (2009): 86–113; Claudia Rapp, "A Medieval Cosmopolis. Constantinople and its Foreign Inhabitants," in *Alexander's Revenge. Hellenistic Culture through the Centuries,* ed. Jón Ma. Asgeirsson and Nancy Van Deusen (Reykjavik: University of Iceland Press, 2002), 162–63.

85 Von Falkenhausen, "In Search of the Jews," 878, with 878–80 on *Adversus Iudaeos* texts; Magdalino, *Empire of Manuel I,* 387.

86 G. Georgiades Arnakis, "Gregory Palamas among the Turks and Documents of his Captivity as Historical Sources," *Speculum* 26 (1951): 104–18.

87 Mary Douglas, *How Institutions Think* (London: Routledge and Kegan Paul, 1987), and see below, Conclusions.

88 Taxonomies, classification and discourse: Bruce Lincoln, *Discourse and the Construction of Society: Comparative Studies of Myth, Ritual and Classification,* 2nd ed. (New York: Oxford University Press, 2014); Mary Douglas, *Leviticus as Literature* (Oxford: Oxford University Press, 1999); Mary

Douglas and David Hull, eds., *How Classification Works: Nelson Goodman among the Social Sciences* (Edinburgh: Edinburgh University Press, 1992).

Conclusions

1   Late medieval dialogues: Carmen Cardelle de Hartmann, *Lateinische Dialoge 12-1400: literaturhistorische Studien und Repertorium* (Leiden: Brill, 2007); Anita Traninger, *Disputation, Deklamation, Dialog. Medien und Gattungen europäischer Wissensverhandlungen zwischen Scholastik und Humanismus*, Text und Kontext 33 (Stuttgart: Franz Steiner Verlag, 2012).

2   For which see Papaioannou, "Voice, signature, mask."

3   Anna Marmodoro and Jonathan Hill, eds., *The Author's Voice in Classical and Late Antiquity* (Oxford: Oxford University Press, 2013), contains three papers dealing with precisely this question in earlier periods.

4   Sarah Culpepper Stroup, "'When I Read my Cato, it is as if Cato Speaks': The Birth and Evolution of Cicero's Dialogic Voice," in Marmadoro and Hill, eds., *The Author's Voice*, 123–51.

5   For instance Virginia Burrus, "'In the Theater of This Life': The Performance of Orthodoxy in Late Antiquity," in *The Limits of Ancient Christianity: Essays on Late Antique Thought and Culture in Honor of R.A. Markus*, ed. William E. Klingshirn and Mark Vessey (Ann Arbor: University of Michigan Press, 1999), 80–96; a similar approach to western medieval scholastic culture: Novikoff, *Medieval Culture*.

6   Kaldellis, "Classical Scholarship."

7   Lieve Van Hoof, "Performing Greek *paideia*: Greek Culture as an Instrument for Social Promotion in the Fourth Century AD," *CQ* 63.1 (2013): 398–99, 402, 405, and see Van Hoof and Van Nuffelen, eds., *Literature and Society in the Fourth Century*; Derek Krueger, *Liturgical Subjects: Christian Ritual, Biblical Narrative and the Formation of Self in Byzantium* (Philadelphia: University of Pennsylvania Press, 2015).

8   Aaron Johnson, "Hellenism and its Discontents," in Scott Fitzgerald Johnson, ed., *The Oxford Handbook of Late Antiquity* (New York and Oxford: Oxford University Press, 2012), 439.

189

9   Papaioannou, *Michael Psellos,* 166–91, on "literary Hellenism," and Hellenism as "a sociolect for the literary elite."

10 Burrus, "'In the theater of this life.'"

11 See chapter two and cf. also Matthew Innes, "Historical Writing, Ethnicity and National Identity: Medieval Europe and Byzantium in Comparison," in Sarah Foot and Chase F. Robinson, eds., *The Oxford Handbook of Historical Writing* 2, 400–1400 (Oxford: Oxford University Press, 2012), 567–68.

12 See Muehlberger, *Angels,* 180 f. on the "imaginative work" that writing has to do.

13 Kendra Eshleman, *The Social World of Intellectuals in the Roman Empire - Sophists, Philosophers and Christians: Greek Culture in the Roman World* (New York: Cambridge University Press, 2012); cf. 261, referring to a "common set of culturally available strategies of self-definition."

14 See Gillian Page, *Being Byzantine: Greek Identity before the Ottomans* (Cambridge: Cambridge University Press, 2008), 67–71.

15 The problems surrounding these poems are many: see Hans Eideneier, *Ptochoprodromos: Einführung, kritische Ausgabe, deutsche Übersetzung, Glossar* (Cologne: Romiosini 1991).

16 Björn Wittrock, "Cultural Crystallization and World History: The Age of Ecumenical Renaissances," *Medieval Encounters* 10.3 (2004): 41–73, provides food for thought on social change, elite formation and social structures from a transnational, Eurasian perspective, though with more on the west than on Byzantium.

17 *Alexiad* X.5; Page, *Being Byzantine,* 42–46.

18 Novikoff, *Medieval Culture.*

19 Krueger, *Liturgical Subjects.*

20 Chapter two above.

21 Muslims as the "other" in the medieval west: Jerold C. Frakes, *Vernacular and Latin Literary Discourses of the Muslim Other in Medieval Germany* (New York: Palgrave Macmillan, 2011).

22 Douglas, *How Institutions Think.*

23 John D. Martin, "Dramatical Disputations: Late Medieval German Dramatizations of Jewish-Christian Religious Disputations, Church Policy and Local Social Climates," *Medieval Encounters* 8.2 (2002): 209–27.

24 Burrus, "'In the Theatre of this Life,'" 96; for the dramatic model see also Erving Goffman, *The Presentation of Self in Everyday Life* (Edinburgh: University of Edinburgh Social Sciences Research Centre, 1956).

25 See Deborah J. Goodwin's move in this direction for the western examples in "'Nothing in *Our* Histories'" (for "Christian identity" see ibid., 39).

26 See also Averil Cameron, *The Byzantines* (Oxford: Wiley-Blackwell, 2006), 15–19.

27 Magdalino, *Empire of Manuel I*, 368.

Abbreviations

193

Bibliography

Abramson, Glenda, and Tudor Parfitt, eds, *Jewish Education and Learning*. London: Harwood Academic Publishers, 1994.

Abulafia, Anna Sapir. *Christians and Jews in the Twelfth-Century Renaissance*. London: Routledge, 1995.

——. *Christians and Jews in Dispute: Disputational Literature and the Rise of Anti-Judaism in the West (c. 1000–1150)*. Aldershot: Variorum, 1998.

——. *Christian-Jewish Relations, 1000–1300: Jews in the Service of Medieval Christendom*. New York: Pearson Education Ltd, 2011.

——. "The Service of Jews in Christian-Jewish Disputations." In Morlet, Munnich and Pouderon, eds. *Les dialogues* Adversus Iudaeos, 339–50.

Adler, Marcus N. *The Itinerary of Benjamin of Tudela: Critical Edition, Translation and Commentary*. New York: P. Feldheim, 1966.

Afentoulidou-Leitgeb, Eirini. "Philippos Monotropos' *Dioptra* and its Social Milieu: Niketas Stethatos, Nikolaos III Grammatikos and the Persecution of Bogomilism." *Parekbolai* 2 (2012): 85–107, accessed March 29, 2015. https://ejournals.lib.auth.gr/parekbolai/

——. "The *Dioptra* of Philippos Monotropos: Didactic Verse or Parody?" In Bernard and Demoen, eds. *Poetry and its Contexts*, 181–94.

Agapitos, Panagiotis A. "Teachers, Pupils and Imperial Power in Eleventh-Century Byzantium." In *Pedagogy and Power: Rhetorics of Classical Learning*, edited by Yun Lee Too and Niall Livingstone, 170–91. Cambridge: Cambridge University Press, 1998.

——. "In Rhomaian, Frankish and Persian Lands: Fiction and Fictionality in Byzantium." In *Medieval Narrative between History and Fiction: From the Centre to the Periphery of Europe, c. 1100–1400*, edited by Panagiotis A. Agapitos and Lars Boje Mortensen, 235–367. Copenhagen: Museum Tusculanum Press, 2012.

Agapitos, Panagiotis, and Dieter Reinsch. *Der Roman im Byzanz in der Komnenenzeit*. Frankfurt am Main: Beerenverlag, 2000.

Akhiezer, Golda. "Byzantine Karaism in the Eleventh to Fifteenth Centuries." In Bonfil, Irshai, Stroumsa, and Talgam, eds. *Jews in Byzantium*, 723–58.

Albini, Umberto. *Michele Psello, Sull'attivita dei demoni*. Genoa: ECIG, 1985.

Alexakis, Alexander. *Codex Parisinus Graecus 1115 and its Archetype*. Washington, DC: Dumbarton Oaks, 1996.

Alexiou, Margaret. "Literary Subversion and the Aristocracy in Twelfth-Century Byzantium: A Stylistic Analysis of the *Timarion*." *BMGS* 8 (1982): 29–45.

——. "The Poverty of *écriture* and the Craft of Writing: Towards a Reappraisal of the Prodromic Poems." *BMGS* 10 (1986): 1–40.

——. "Ploys of Performance: Games and Play in the Ptochoprodromic Poems." *DOP* 53 (1999): 91–109.

——. *After Antiquity: Greek Language, Myth and Metaphor*. Ithaca, NY: University of Cornell Press, 2002.

——. "Afterword: Literary Subversion in Byzantium." In Angelov and Saxby, eds. *Power and Subversion*, 281–88.

Amato, Eugenio, with Alexandre Roduit and Martin Steinrück, eds. *Approches de la Troisième Sophistique, Hommages à Jacques Schamp* (Brussels: Editions Latomus, 2006).

Anderson, Glaire D. "Islamic Spaces and Diplomacy in Constantinople (Tenth to Thirteenth Centuries C.E.)." *Medieval Encounters* 15.1 (2009): 86–113.

Andrist, Patrick. "The Greek Bible Used by the Jews in the Dialogues *Contra Iudaeos* (Fourth-Tenth Centuries CE)." In *Jewish Receptions of Greek Bible Versions: Studies in their Use in Late Antiquity and the*

Middle Ages, edited by Nicholas de Lange, Julia G. Krivoruchko and Cameron Boyd-Taylor, 235–61. Tübingen: Mohr Siebeck, 2009.

——. "The Physiognomy of Greek *Contra Iudaeos* Manuscript Books in the Byzantine Era: A Preliminary Survey," in Bonfil, Irshai, Stroumsa and Targam, eds. *Jews in Byzantium*, 549–85.

Angelov, Dimiter, and Michael Saxby, eds. *Power and Subversion in Byzantium*. Farnham: Ashgate, 2013.

Angold, Michael. *Church and Society under the Comneni 1081–1261*. Cambridge: Cambridge University Press, 1995.

——, ed. *The Byzantine Aristocracy, IX to XIII Centuries*. Oxford: B.A.R., 1984.

Argyriou, Asterios. "Perception de l'Islam et traductions du Coran dans le monde byzantin grec." *Byzantion* 75 (2005): 25–69.

Arnakis, G. Georgiades. "Gregory Palamas among the Turks and Documents of his Captivity as Historical Sources," *Speculum* 26 (1951): 104–18.

Arnason, Johann P. "Byzantium and Historical Sociology." In Stephenson, ed. *The Byzantine* World, 491–504.

Arnason, Johann P. and Bjorn Wittrock, eds, *Medieval Encounters* 10 (2004)

Asad, Talal. *Genealogies of Religion: Discipline and Reasons of Power in Christianity and Islam*. Baltimore: Johns Hopkins University Press, 1993.

Asgeirsson, Jón Ma., and Nancy Van Deusen, eds. *Alexander's Revenge. Hellenistic Culture through the Centuries*. Reykjavik: University of Iceland Press, 2002.

Astruc, Charles, Wanda Conus-Wolska, Jean Gouillard, Paul Lemerle, Denise Papachryssanthou, and Jean Paramelle. "Les sources grecques pour l'histoire des Pauliciens d'Asie Mineure: texte critique et traduction." *Travaux et Mémoires* 4 (1970): 1–227.

Augé, Isabelle. *Byzantins, Arméniens et Francs au temps de la croisade. Politique religieuse et reconquête en Orient sous la dynastie des Comnènes, 1081–1185*. Paris: S.N. Librairie Orientale Paul Geuthner, 2007.

——. *Églises en dialogue: Arméniens et Byzantins dans la seconde moitié du XIIe siècle*. CSCO 633, Subsidia 124. Louvain: Peeters, 2011.

197

Aulisa, Immacolata. *Guidei e cristiani nell'agiografia dell'alto Medioevo.* Bari: Edipuglia, 2009.

——. "La polemica *adversus Iudaeos* nell'agiografia dell'alto medioevo," In Morlet, Munnich, Pouderon, eds. *Les dialogues* Adversus Iudaeos, 269–94.

Balard, Michel, and Alain Ducellier. *Migrations et diasporas m*éditerranéennes (Xe–*XVIe siècles).* Paris: Publications de la Sorbonne, 2002.

Baldwin, Barry. *Timarion.* Detroit: Wayne State University Press, 1984.

Bang, Peter Fibiger, and Dariusz Kolodziejczyk, eds. *Universal Empire: A Comparative Approach to Imperial Culture and Representation in Eurasian History.* Cambridge: Cambridge University Press, 2012.

Bang, Peter Fibiger, and Walter Scheidel, eds. *The Oxford Handbook of the State in the Ancient Near East and Mediterranean.* Oxford: Oxford University Press, 2013.

Barber, Charles. *Contesting the Logic of Painting: Art and Understanding in Eleventh-Century Byzantium.* Leiden: Brill, 2007.

Barber, Charles, and David Jenkins, eds. *Medieval Greek Commentaries on the Nicomachean Ethics.* Leiden: Brill, 2009.

Beaton, Roderick. "The Rhetoric of Poverty: The Lives and Opinions of Theodore Prodromos." *BMGS* 11 (1987): 1–28.

——. *The Medieval Greek Romance.* 2nd rev. ed. London: Routledge, 1996.

——. "Antique Nation? 'Hellenes' on the Eve of Independence and in Twelfth-Century Byzantium." *BMGS* 31.1 (2007): 76–85.

Beck, Hans-Georg. *Kirche und theologische Literatur im byzantinischen Reich.* Munich: C.H. Beck'sche Verlagsbuchhandlung, 1959.

Becker, Adam H. "The Discourse of Priesthood (BL Add. 18295, ff. 137b–140b): An Anti-Jewish Text on the Abrogation of the Israelite Priesthood." *JSS* 51.1 (2006): 85–115.

Berger, Albrecht, ed. *Life and Works of Saint Gregentios, Archbishop of Taphar: Introduction, Critical Edition and Translation.* Berlin: de Gruyter, 2006.

Berger, David. "Mission to the Jews and Christian-Jewish Contacts in the Polemical Literature of the High Middle Ages." *AHR* 91 (1986): 576–91.

Berger, Peter, and Thomas Luckmann. *The Social Construction of Reality: A Treatise in the Sociology of Knowledge*. London: Penguin, 1967.

Bernard, Floris. *Writing and Reading Byzantine Secular Poetry, 1025–81*. Oxford: Oxford University Press, 2014.

Bernard, Floris, and Kristoffel Demoen, eds. *Poetry and its Contexts in Eleventh-Century Byzantium*. Farnham: Ashgate, 2012.

Bio, Anna Ieraci, "Il dialogo nella letteratura bizantina." In *Spirito e forma della letteratura bizantina: Actes de la séance plénière d'ouverture du XXe Congrès international des études byzantines, Paris, 19–25 août, 2001*, edited by Antonio Garzya, 21–45. Naples: Quaderni dell'accademia pontaniana 47, 2006.

Blanks, David R. "Western Views of Islam in the Premodern Period: A Brief History of Past Approaches." In Frassetto and Blanks, eds. *Western Views of Islam*, 11–53.

Blumenkranz, Bernhard. *Les auteurs chrétiens latins du moyen âge sur les juifs et le judaïsme*. Paris: Mouton, 1963, 2nd ed. Paris–Louvain: Peeters, 2007.

Bonfil, Robert. "Continuity and Discontinuity (641–1204)." In Bonfil, Irshai, Stroumsa and Talgam, eds. *Jews in Byzantium*, 65–100.

Bonfil, Robert, Oded Irshai, Guy G. Stroumsa, and Rina Talgam, eds. *Jews in Byzantium: Dialectics of Minority and Majority Cultures*. Leiden: Brill, 2012.

Bossina, Luciano. "L'eresia dopo la crociata. Niceta Coniate, i Latini e gli azimi (*Panoplia Dogmatica* XXII)." In *Padri Greci e Latini a Confronto (secoli XIII–XV)*, edited by Mariarosa Cortesi, 154–205. Firenze: SISMEL - Edizioni del Galluzzo, 2004.

——. "Niketas Choniates as a Theologian." In *Niketas Choniates: A Historian and a Writer*, edited by Alicia Simpson and Stephanos Efthymiades, 165–84. Geneva: La Pomme d'Or, 2009.

Bourbouhakis, Emmanuel C. "Rhetoric and Performance." In Stephenson, ed. *The Byzantine World*, 175–87.

——. "The End of ἐπίδειξις: Authorial Identity and Authorial Intention in Michael Choniatēs' Πρὸς τοὺς αἰτιωμένους τὸ φιλένδεικτον." In Pizzone, ed. *The Author in Middle Byzantine Literature*, 201–24.

Bourdieu, Pierre. *Outline of a Theory of Practice*. Cambridge, Cambridge University Press, 1977.

——. *Distinction: A Social Critique of the Judgement of Taste*. London: Routledge, 1984.

——. *Homo Academicus*. Cambridge: Polity Press, 1988.

——. *Language and Symbolic Power*. Cambridge: Polity Press, 1991.

——. *The Field of Cultural Production*. Cambridge: Polity Press, 1993.

Bowman, Steven. *The Jews of Byzantium, 1204–1453*. Atlanta: University of Alabama Press, 1985.

——. "Twelfth-Century Jewish Responses to Crusade and *jihad*." In *Crusaders, Condottieri and Cannon: Medieval Warfare in Societies around the Mediterranean*, edited by Donald J. Kagay and L. J. Andrew Villalon, 417–38. Leiden: Brill, 2003.

Brakke, David, Deborah Deliyannis, and Edward Watts, eds. *Shifting Cultural Frontiers in Late Antiquity*. Farnham: Ashgate, 2012.

Browning, Robert. "Enlightenment and Repression in Byzantium in the Eleventh and Twelfth Centuries." *Past and Present* 69 (1975): 3–23.

Buckley, Penelope. *The* Alexiad *of Anna Komnene: Artistic Strategy in the Making of Myth*. Cambridge: Cambridge University Press, 2014.

Bucossi, Alessandra. "George Skylitzes' Dedicatory Verses for the *Sacred Arsenal* by Andronikos Kamateros and the Codex Marcianus Graecus 524." *JÖB* 59 (2009): 37–50.

——. "The *Sacred Arsenal* by Andronikos Kamateros: A Forgotten Treasure." In Rigo and Ermilov, eds. *Byzantine Theologians*, 33–50.

——. "New Historical Evidence for the Dating of the *Sacred Arsenal* by Andronikos Kamateros." *REB* 67 (2009): 111–30.

——. "Dialogues and Anthologies of the *Sacred Arsenal* by Andronikos Kamateros: Sources, Arrangements, Purposes." In *Encyclopaedic Trends in Byzantium*, edited by Peter van Deun and Caroline Macé, 269–86. Orientalia Lovaniensia Analecta 21. Peeters: Leuven, 2011.

——. *Andronici Camateri Sacrum Armamentarium, Pars Prima*, CCSG 75. Turnhout: Brepols, 2014.

——. "The Six Dialogues by Niketa 'of Maroneia': An Introduction." In Cameron and Gaul, eds. *Dialogues and Debates*, forthcoming.

Burke, Peter J., and Jan E. Stets. *Identity Theory*. New York: Oxford University Press, 2009.

Burman, Thomas E. *Reading the Qur'an in Latin Christendom, 1140–1560*. Philadelphia: University of Pennsylvania Press, 2007.

Burrus, Virginia. "'In the Theater of this Life': The Performance of Orthodoxy in Late Antiquity." In *The Limits of Ancient Christianity: Essays on Late Antique Thought and Culture in Honor of R. A. Markus*, edited by William E. Klingshirn and Mark Vessey, 80–96. Ann Arbor: University of Michigan Press, 1999.

Burton, Joan B. "Byzantine Readers." In *The Cambridge Companion to the Greek and Roman Novel*, edited by Tim Whitmarsh, 272–81. Cambridge: Cambridge University Press, 2008.

Bussières, Marie-Pierre, ed., *La littérature des questions et réponses dans l'Antiquité profane et chrétienne: de l'enseignement à l'exégèse*. Actes du séminaire sur le genre des questions et réponses tenu à Ottawa les 27 et 28 septembre 2009. Instrumenta Patristica et Mediaevalia 64. Turnhout: Brepols, 2011.

Bydén, Börje. "'Strangle them with the Meshes of Syllogisms!': Latin Philosophy in Greek Translations of the Thirteenth Century." In *Interaction and Isolation in Late Byzantine Culture: Papers read at a colloquium held at the Swedish Research Institute in Istanbul, 1–5 December, 1999*, edited by Jan Olof Rosenqvist, 133–57. Transactions of the Swedish Research Institute in Istanbul 13. Stockholm: Swedish Research Institute in Istanbul, 2004.

Bydén, Börje, and Katerina Ierodiakonou, eds. *The Many Faces of Byzantine Philosophy*. Athens: Norwegian Institute at Athens, 2012.

Cain, Andrew, and Noel Lenski, eds. *The Power of Religion in Late Antiquity*. Farnham: Ashgate, 2009.

Cameron, Averil. "Jews and Heretics – a Category Error?" In *The Ways that Never Parted: Jews and Christians in Late Antiquity and the Early Middle Ages*, edited by Adam H. Becker and Annette Yoshiko Reed, 345–60. Tübingen: Mohr Siebeck, 2003.

———. "How to Read Heresiology." *Journal of Medieval and Early Modern Studies* 33.3 (Fall, 2003): 471–92. Also in *The Cultural Turn in Late Ancient Studies: Gender, Asceticism and Historiography*, edited by Dale

201

B. Martin and Patricia Cox Miller, 193–212. Durham, NC: Duke University Press, 2005.

——. *The Byzantines*. Oxford: Wiley-Blackwell, 2006.

——. "Enforcing Orthodoxy in Byzantium." In *Discipline and Diversity*, edited by Kate Cooper and Jeremy Gregory, 1–24. Studies in Church History 43. Woodbridge: Ecclesiastical History Society, 2007.

——. "Thinking with Byzantium." *Transactions of the Royal Historical Society* 21 (2011): 39–57.

——. *Byzantine Matters*. Princeton: Princeton University Press, 2014.

——. *Dialoguing in Late Antiquity*. Hellenic Studies Series 65. Washington, DC: Centre for Hellenic Studies, 2014.

——. "Christian Literature and Christian History." Hans-Lietzmann-Vorlesung 2013. Berlin: de Gruyter, forthcoming.

Cameron, Averil, and Robert Hoyland, eds. *Doctrine and Debate in the East Christian World, 300–1500*. Farnham: Ashgate, 2011.

Cameron, Averil, and Niels Gaul, eds., *Dialogues and Debates from Late Antiquity to Late Byzantium*, forthcoming.

Caseau, Béatrice. *Byzance: économie et société. Du milieu du VIIIe siècle à 1204*. Paris: Sedes, 2007.

Chadwick, Henry. *East and West: The Making of a Rift within the Church*. Oxford: Oxford University Press, 2003.

Charalampopoulos, N. G. "A Platonic Dialogue of the Twelfth Century: Theodore Prodromos's *Xenedemos* or *Voices*." *Ariadne* 11 (2005): 189–214 (in Greek).

Chazan, Robert. "Twelfth-Century Perceptions of the Jews: A Case Study of Bernard of Clairvaux and Peter the Venerable." In *From Witness to Witchcraft: Jews and Judaism in Medieval Christian Thought*, edited by Jeremy Cohen, 187–201. Wolfenbütteler Mittelalter-Studien 11. Wiesbaden: Harassowitz Verlag, 1996.

Chitoiu, Dan. "Ideology and Philosophy in Byzantium: The Meanings of Ideology before Modern Times." *Journal for the Study of Religions and Ideologies* 8.23 (2009): 48–67.

Chrontz, M., ed. *Νεκταρίου, ἡγουμένου μονῆς Κασούλων Νικολάου Ὑδρουντινοῦ, Διάλεξις κατὰ Ἰουδαίων*. Athens, 2009.

Clark, Elizabeth A., *History, Theory, Text: Historians and the Linguistic Turn*. Cambridge, Mass.: Harvard University Press, 2004.

——, "The Retrospective Self," *The Catholic Historical Review* 101.1 (2015): 1–27.

Cohen, Jeremy. "Scholarship and Intolerance in the Medieval Academy: The Study and Evaluation of Judaism in European Christendom." *AHR* 91 (1986): 592–613. Reprinted in Cohen, ed., *Essential Papers on Judaism and Christianity in Conflict*, 310–41.

——, ed. *Essential Papers on Judaism and Christianity in Conflict, from Late Antiquity to the Reformation*. New York: New York University Press, 1991.

——. "Towards a Functional Classification of Jewish Anti-Christian Polemic in the High Middle Ages." In *Religionsgespräche im Mittelalter*, edited by Bernard Lewis and Friedrich Niewöhner, 93–114. Wiesbaden: Harassowitz, 1992.

Cook, Michael. "The Origins of *kalam*." *Bulletin of the School of Oriental and African Studies* 43.1 (1980): 32–43.

Coppola, Mario, Germana Fernicola and Lucia Pappalardo, eds. *Dialogus. Il dialogo fra le religioni nel pensiero tardo-antico, medievale e umanistico*. Rome: Città Nuova, 2014.

Corrigan, Kathleen. *Visual Polemics in the Ninth-Century Byzantine Psalters*. Cambridge: Cambridge University Press, 1992.

Criste, Ambrose, and Carol Need. *Anselm of Havelberg, Anticimenon: On the Unity of Faith and the Controversies with the Greeks*. Collegeville, Minn., 2010.

Crostini, Barbara. "Christianity and Judaism in Eleventh-Century Constantinople." In *Eukosmia. Studi miscellanei per il 75º di Vincenzo Poggi S.J.*, edited by Vincenzo Ruggieri and Luca Pieralli, 169–87. Soveria Mannelli, CZ: Rubbettino, 2003.

——, "Augustine in the Byzantine World to 1453." In *The Oxford Guide to the Reception of Augustine*, edited by Karla Pollman, vol II, 726–34. 3 vols. Oxford: Oxford University Press, 2013.

Dahan, Gilbert. *The Christian Polemic against Jews in the Middle Ages*. Notre Dame: University of Notre Dame Press, 1998.

——. "Les questions d'exégèse dans les dialogues contre les juifs, XIIe-XIIIe siècles." In Morlet, Munnich and Pouderon, eds. *Les dialogues* Adversus Iudaeos, 319–38.

Dagron, Gilbert. "Minorités ethniques et religieuses dans l'orient byzantin à la fin du X et au XI siècle: l'immigration syrienne." *Travaux et Mémoires* 6 (1976): 177–216.

——. "Le traité de Grégoire de Nicée sur le baptême des Juifs." *Travaux et Mémoires* 11 (1991): 313–57.

Darrouzès, Jean. "Les conférences de 1112." *REB* 23 (1965): 51–55.

——. "Les documents byzantins du XIIe siècle sur la primauté romaine." *REB* 23 (1965): 51–59.

——. *Documents inédits d'ecclésiologie byzantine*. Paris: Institut français d'études byzantines, 1966.

Davis, Natalie Zemon. *Women on the Margins: Three Seventeenth-Century Lives*. Cambridge, Mass: Harvard University Press, 1995.

——. *Trickster Travels: A Sixteenth-Century Muslim Between Worlds*. New York: Hill and Wang, 2006.

——. "Decentering History: Local Stories and Cultural Crossings in a Global World." *History and Theory* 50 (2011): 188–202.

de Lange, Nicholas, "A Fragment of Byzantine Anti-Christian Polemic." *JJS* 41 (1990): 92–100.

——, "Byzantium in the Cairo Genizah," *BMGS* 16 (1992): 34–47.

——. "Jewish Education in the Byzantine Empire in the Twelfth Century." In *Jewish Education and Learning*, edited by Glenda Abramson and Tudor Parfitt, 115–28. London: Harwood Academic Publishers, 1994.

——, ed. *Hebrew Scholarship and the Medieval World*, 23–37. Cambridge: Cambridge University Press, 2008.

——. "Hebrew Scholarship in Byzantium." In *Hebrew Scholarship and the Medieval World*, edited by Nicholas de Lange, 23–37.

——. "Hebrew Inscriptions of the Byzantine Empire." In *Manuscrits hébreux et arabes. Mélanges en l'honneur de Colette Sirat*, edited by Nicholas de Lange and Judith Olszowy-Schlanger, 415–24. Bibliologia 38. Turnhout: Brepols, 2014.

Demacopoulos, George E., and Aristotle Papanikolaou, eds. *Orthodox Constructions of the West*. New York: Fordham University Press, 2013.

Demetrakopoulos, A., *Ekklesiastike Bibliotheke*. Leipzig, Othon Bigandos, 1866. Reprint, Hildesheim: Olms, 1965.

Domínguez, Oscar Prieto. "The Mass Conversion of Jews Decreed by Emperor Basil I in 873–74: Its Reflection in Contemporary Legal Codes and its Underlying Reasons." In *Jews in Early Christian Law: Byzantium and the West, 6th to 11th Centuries*, edited by John Tolan, Nicholas de Lange, Laurence Foschia and Capucine Nemo-Pekelman, 283–310. Turnhout: Brepols, 2013.

Dondaine, Antoine. "Hugues Éthérien et Léon Toscan." *Archives de l'histoire doctrinales et littéraires du Moyen Âge* 19 (1952): 473–83.

——. "Hugues Ethérien et le concile de Constantinople de 1166." *Historisches Jahrbuch* 77 (1958): 473–83.

Douglas, Mary. *How Institutions Think*. London: Routledge and Kegan Paul, 1987.

——, *Leviticus as Literature*. Oxford: Oxford University Press, 1999.

Douglas, Mary, and David Hull, eds. *How Classification Works: Nelson Goodman among the Social Sciences*. Edinburgh: Edinburgh University Press, 1992.

Dubel, Sandrine, and Sophie Gotteland, eds. *Formes et genres du dialogue antique*. Scripta Antiqua 71. Bordeaux: Éditions Ausonius, 2015.

Ducellier, Alain. *Chrétiens d'Orient et l'Islam au Moyen Âge, VIIe–XVe siècle*. Paris: Armand Colin/Masson, 1996.

Eichner, Wolfgang. "Byzantine Accounts of Islam." In Cameron and Hoyland, eds. *Doctrine and Debate*, 109–70.

Eideneier, Hans. *Ptochoprodromos: Einführung, kritische Ausgabe, deutsche Übersetzung, Glossar*. Cologne: Romiosini, 1991.

Eleuteri, Paolo, and Antonio Rigo. *Eretici, dissidenti, musulmani ed ebrei a Bisanzio: una raccolta eresiologica del XII secolo*. Venice: Il Cardo, 1993.

Eshleman, Kendra. *The Social World of Intellectuals in the Roman Empire: Sophists, Philosophers, and Christians. Greek Culture in the Roman World*. New York: Cambridge University Press, 2012.

Falkenhausen, Vera von. "The Jews in Byzantine Southern Italy." In Bonfil, Irshai, Stroumsa and Talgam, eds. *Jews in Byzantium*, 271–96.

——. "In Search of the Jews in Byzantine Literature." In Bonfil, Irshai, Stroumsa, Targam, eds. *Jews in Byzantium*, 871–91.

Ferruolo, Stephen C. "The Twelfth-Century Renaissance." In *Renaissances before the Renaissance: Cultural Revivals of Late Antiquity and the Middle Ages*, edited by Warren T. Treadgold, 114–43. Stanford: Stanford University Press, 1984.

Förstel, K. *Schriften contre l'Islam (8e–13e siècle)*. Altenberge: Oros, 1982.

——. *Niketas von Byzanz. Schriften zum Islam*. Würzburg: Echter, 2000.

——. *Schriften zum Islam von Arethas und Euthymios Zigabenos und Fragmente der griechischen Koranübersetzung*. Wiesbaden: Harassowitz, 2009.

Fowden, Garth. *Before and After Muhammad: The First Millenium Refocused*. Princeton: Princeton University Press, 2014.

Fowler, Ryan C., and Alberto J. Quiroga Puertas, "A Prolegomena to the Third Sophistic." In *Plato in the Third Sophistic*, edited by Ryan C. Fowler, 1–30. Berlin: De Gruyter, 2014.

Frakes, Jerold C. *Vernacular and Latin Literary Discourses of the Muslim Other in Medieval Germany*. New York: Palgrave Macmillan, 2011.

Frankopan, Peter. *The First Crusade: The Call from the East*. London: Bodley Head, 2012.

——. "The Literary, Cultural and Philosophical Context for the Twelfth-Century Commentary on the Nicomachean Ethics." In Barber and Jenkins, eds. *Medieval Greek Commentaries*, 45–62.

Frassetto, Michael, and David R. Blanks, eds. *Western Views of Islam in Medieval and Early Modern Europe*. Basingstoke: Macmillan, 1999.

Frederiksen, Paula. *Augustine and the Jews: A Christian Defense of Jews and Judaism*. 2nd ed. with Postscript. New Haven: Yale University Press, 2010.

Frugoni, Arsenio. Adversus Iudaeos *di Gioacchino da Fiore*. Rome: Nella sede dell'Istituto, 1957.

Gaul, Niels. *Thomas Magistros und die spätbyzantinische Sophistik. Studien zum Humanismus urbaner Eliten in der frühen Palaiologenzeit*. Mainzer Veröffentlichungen zur Byzantinistik 10. Wiesbaden: Harasowitz Verlag, 2011.

——. "Rising Elites and Institutionalization – *Ethos/Mores* – 'Debts' and Drafts: Three Concluding Steps towards Comparing Networks of Learning in Byzantium and the 'Latin' West, c. 1000–1200." In Steckel, Gaul and Grünbart, eds. *Networks of Learning*, 235–80.

Gautier, Paul. "Le *De daemonibus* du Pseudo-Psellos." *REB* 38 (1980): 105–94.

George-Tvrtković, Rita. *A Christian Pilgrim in Medieval Iraq: Riccoldo da Montecroce's Encounter with Islam.* Turnhout: Brepols, 2012.

Goffman, Erving. *The Presentation of Self in Everyday Life.* Edinburgh: University of Edinburgh Social Sciences Research Centre, 1956.

Goodwin, Deborah J. "'Nothing in *Our* Histories': A Post-Colonial Perspective on Twelfth-Century Christian Hebraism." *Medieval Encounters* 15.1 (2009): 35–65.

Gouma-Peterson, Thalia. *Anna Komnene and Her Times.* New York: Garland Publishing, 2000.

Griffith, Sidney H. *The Church in the Shadow of the Mosque: Christians and Muslims in the World of Islam.* Princeton, NJ: Princeton University Press, 2008.

Grumel, Venance. "Autour du voyage de Pierre Grossolano, archévêque de Milan à Constantinople en 1112." Échos d'Orient 32 (1933): 22–33.

Grünbart, Michael. "'Tis Love that has Warm'd Us': Reconstructing Networks in Twelfth-Century Byzantium." *Revue belge de philologie et d'histoire* 83.2 (2005): 301–13.

Grünbart, Michael, ed. *Theatron: rhetorische Kultur in Spätantike und Mittelalter.* Berlin: De Gruyter, 2007.

Haldon, John F. "The Byzantine Empire." In *The Dynamics of Ancient Empires*, edited by Ian Morris and Walter Scheidel, 224–73. Oxford: Oxford University Press, 2009.

——. "Towards a Social History of Byzantium." In Haldon, ed., *A Social History of Byzantium*, 1–30.

——. "The Byzantine Successor State." In *The Oxford Handbook of the State in the Ancient Near East and Mediterranean*, edited by Peter Fibiger Bang and Walter Scheidel, 475–97. Oxford: Oxford University Press, 2013.

207

———. ed. *A Social History of Byzantium*. Chichester: Wiley-Blackwell, 2009.

Haldon, John F., and Lawrence I. Conrad, eds. *Elites Old and New in the Islamic and Early Byzantine Near East*. Sixth Workshop, Studies in Late Antiquity and Early Islam, Byzantium and the Early Islamic Near East. Princeton, NJ: Darwin Press, 1999.

Hamilton, Janet, Sarah Hamilton, and Bernard Hamilton. *Hugh Eteriano: Contra Patarenos*. Leiden: Brill, 2004.

Hanson, Craig L. "Manuel I Comnenus and the 'God of Muhammad': A Study in Byzantine Ecclesiastical Politics." In *Medieval Perceptions of Islam*, edited by John Tolan, 55–84. London: Routledge, 1996.

Harboun, Haïm. *Les voyageurs juifs du XIIe siècle: Benjamin de Tudèle, 1165/66–1172/73*. Aix-en-Provence: Éditions Massoreth, 1998.

Harris, Jonathan, Catherine Holmes, and Eugenia Russell, eds. *Byzantines, Latins, and Turks in the Mediterranean World after 1150*. Oxford: Oxford University Press, 2012.

Hartmann, Carmen Cardelle de. *Lateinische Dialoge 1200–1400: literaturhistorische Studien und Repertorium*. Leiden: Brill, 2007.

Hinterberger, Martin, ed. *The Language of Byzantine Learned Literature*. Turnhout: Brepols, 2014.

Hirschfeld, Hartwig. *Judah Hallevi's* Kitab al Khazari. Rev. ed. London: M. L. Callingold, 1931.

Hoeck, Johannes M., and Raimund J. Loenertz. *Nikolaos-Nektarios von Otranto, Abt von Casole. Beiträge zur Geschichte der ost-westlichen Beziehungen unter Innocent III und Friedrich II*. Ettal: Buch-Kunstverlag Ettal, 1965.

Holmes, Catherine. "Shared Worlds: Religious Identities – a Question of Evidence." In Harris, Holmes and Russell, eds. *Byzantines, Latins, and Turks*, 31–60.

Hörandner, Wolfram. "Zur kommunikativen Funktion byzantinischer Gedichte." Acts, XVIIIth International Congress of Byzantine Studies, Selected Papers IV, 104–18. Shepherdstown, 1996.

Horbury, William. "Hebrew Apologetic and Polemical Literature." In de Lange, ed. *Hebrew Scholarship and the Medieval World*, 189–209.

208

Hösle, Vittorio. *The Philosophical Dialogue*. Eng. trans. Notre Dame, Ind.: University of Notre Dame Press, 2012.

Hoyland, Robert. *Seeing Islam as Others Saw It: A Survey and Evaluation of Christian, Jewish and Zoroastrian Writings on Early Islam*. Studies in Late Antiquity and Early Islam 13. Princeton, NJ: Darwin Press, 1997.

Hunger, Herbert. *Der byzantinische Katz-Mäuse-Krieg*. Graz-Vienna-Cologne: Böhlau, 1968.

Hunger, Herbert. "On the Imitation (ΜΙΜΗΣΙΣ) of Antiquity in Byzantine Literature." *DOP* 23/24 (1969/70): 15–38.

Ierodiakonou, Katerina, ed. *Byzantine Philosophy and its Ancient Sources*. Oxford: Oxford University Press, 2002.

Innes, Matthew. "Historical Writing, Ethnicity and National Identity: Medieval Europe and Byzantium in Comparison." In *The Oxford History of Historical Writing 2, 400–1400*, edited by Sarah Foot and Chase F. Robinson, 539–74. Oxford: Oxford University Press, 2012).

Ioannou, P. "Le sort des évêques hérétiques réconciliés: le discours inédit de Nicétas de Serres contre Eustrate de Nicée." *Byzantion* 28 (1958): 1–30.

Iogna-Prat, Dominique. *Order and Exclusion: Cluny and Christendom Face Heresy, Judaism and Islam (1000–1150)*. Ithaca, NY: Cornell University Press, 2002.

Jacoby, David. "Les quartiers juifs à Constantinople à l'époque byzantine." *Byzantion* 37 (1967): 167–227. Repr. in David Jacoby, *Société et démographie à Byzance et en Romanie latine*. London: Variorum, 1975, no. II.

——. "The Jews of Constantinople and their Demographic Hinterland." In *Constantinople and its Hinterland*, edited by Cyril Mango and Gilbert Dagron, 221–232. Aldershot: Variorum, 1995. Repr. in David Jacoby, *Byzantium, Latin Romania and the Mediterranean*. Aldershot: Ashgate, 2001, no. IV.

——. "The Jewish Community in Constantinople from the Komnenan to the Palaiologan Period." *Vizantijski Vremennik* 55 (1998): 31–40. Repr. in *Byzantium, Latin Romania and the Mediterranean*, no. V.

——. "The Jews and the Silk Industry of Constantinople." In David Jacoby, *Byzantium, Latin Romania and the Mediterranean*, no. XI.

——. "Benjamin of Tudela in Byzantium." *Palaeoslavica* 10 (2002): 18–85.

209

——. "Foreigners and the Urban Economy in Thessalonike, ca. 1150–ca. 1450." *DOP* 57 (2003): 85–132.

——. "Benjamin of Tudela and his Book of Travels." In *Venezia, incrocio di culture*, edited by Klaus Herbers and Felicitas Schmieder, 1000–1030. Rome: Edizioni di storia e letteratura, 2008.

James, Liz, ed. *A Companion to Byzantium*. Chichester: Wiley-Blackwell, 2010.

Jeffreys, Elizabeth M. "The Comnenian Background to the *romans de l'antiquité*." *Byzantion* 50 (1980): 455–86. Repr. in Elizabeth Jeffreys and Michael Jeffreys. *Popular Literature in Late Byzantium*, no. X. .London: Variorum, 1983.

——. "Why Produce Verse in Twelfth-Century Constantinople?" In Odorico, Agapitos, and Hinterberger, eds. *Doux remède*, 219–28.

——. *Four Byzantine Novels*. Liverpool: Liverpool University Press, 2012.

——. "We Need to Talk about Byzantium: or, Byzantium, its Reception of the Classical World as Discussed in Current Scholarship, and Should Classicists Pay Attention?" *Classical Receptions Journal* 6.1 (2014): 158–74.

——. "The Sebastokratorissa Irene as Patron." In *Female Founders in Byzantium and Beyond*, edited by Lioba Theis, Margaret Mullett, Michael Grünbart, Galina Fingarova and Matthew Savage, 177–94. Köln-Weimar-Wien: Böhlau Verlag, 2014.

Jeffreys, Michael J. "The Literary Emergence of Vernacular Greek." *Mosaic* 8.4 (1975): 171–93.

——. "Early Modern Greek Verse: Parallels and Frameworks." *Modern Greek Studies (Australia and New Zealand)* 1 (2012): 49–78.

Johnson, Aaron P. "Hellenism and its Discontents." In *The Oxford Handbook of Late Antiquity*, edited by Scott Fitzgerald Johnson, 436–56. New York and Oxford: Oxford University Press, 2012.

Johnson, Christopher D. L. "'He Has Made the Dry Bones Live': Orientalism's Attempted Resuscitation of Eastern Christianity." *Journal of the American Academy of Religion* 82.3 (2014): 811–40.

Kaldellis, Anthony. *Hellenism in Byzantium: The Transformations of Greek Identity and the Reception of the Classical Tradition*. Cambridge: Cambridge University Press, 2007.

———. "The Corpus of Byzantine Historiography: An Interpretive Essay." In Stephenson, ed., *The Byzantine World*, 213–22.

———. "The Byzantine Role in the Making of the Corpus of Classical Greek Historiography: A Preliminary Investigation." *JHS* 132 (2012): 71–85.

———. "The *Timarion*: Towards a Literary Description." In Odorico, ed. *La face cachée*, 275–87.

———. "Classical Scholarship in Twelfth-Century Byzantium." In Barber and Jenkins, eds. *Medieval Commentaries*, 1–44.

Karamanolis, George. "Form and Content in the Dialogues of Gennadios Scholarios." In Cameron and Gaul, eds., *Dialogues and Debates*, forthcoming.

Kazhdan, Alexander, and Giles Constable. *People and Power in Byzantium: An Introduction to Modern Byzantine Studies*. Washington, DC: Dumbarton Oaks, 1982.

Kazhdan, Alexander P., in collaboration with Simon Franklin. *Studies on the Byzantine Literature of the Eleventh and Twelfth Centuries*. Cambridge: Cambridge University Press, 1984.

Kazhdan, Alexander P., and Ann Wharton Epstein. *Change in Byzantine Culture in the Eleventh and Twelfth Centuries*. Berkeley and Los Angeles: University of California Press, 1985.

Kazhdan, Alexander P., and Silvia Ronchey. *L'aristocrazia bizantina dal principio dell'XI alla fine del XII secolo*. Palermo: Sellerio 1997.

Khoury, Adel T. *Les théologiens byzantins et l'Islam. Textes et auteurs, VIIIe–XIIIe siècle*. Beyrouth–Louvain, 1969.

———. *Apologétique byzantine contre l'Islam (8e–13e siècles)*. Attenberg: Verlag für Christlich-Islamisches Schrifttum, 1982.

Kolbaba, Tia M. *The Byzantine Lists: Errors of the Latins*. Urbana, Ill.: University of Illinois Press, 2000.

———. "Byzantine Perceptions of Latin Religious 'Errors.'" In Laiou and Mottahadeh, eds. *The Crusades from the Perspective of Byzantium and the Muslim World*, 117–43.

———. "The Orthodoxy of the Latins in the Twelfth Century." In *Byzantine Orthodoxies*, edited by Andrew Louth and Augustine Casiday, 199–214.

211

Society for the Promotion of Byzantine Studies Publications 12. Aldershot: Ashgate, 2006.

——. *Inventing Latin Heretics: Byzantines and the Filioque in the Ninth Century*. Kalamazoo: Medieval Institute Publications, Western Michigan, 2008.

——. "Byzantines, Armenians, Latins: Unleavened Bread and Heresy in the Tenth Century." In Demacopoulos and Papanikolaou, eds. *Orthodox Constructions of the West*, 45–56.

Komnene, Anna. *The Alexiad*. Trans. E.R.A. Sewter. Revised with Introduction and Notes by Peter Frankopan. London: Penguin, 2009.

Korobeinikov, Dimitri. "A Sultan in Constantinople: The Feasts of Ghiyāth al-Dīn Kay-Khusraw I." In *Eat, Drink and be Merry (Luke 12:19): Food and Wine in Byzantium*, edited by Leslie Brubaker and Kallirroe Linardou, 93–108. Aldershot: Ashgate, 2007.

Krallis, Dimitris. "Harmless Satire, Stinging Critique: Notes and Suggestions for Reading the *Timarion*." In Angelov and Saxby, eds, *Power and Subversion*, 221–45.

Krauss, Samuel, and William Horbury. *The Jewish-Christian Controversy from the Earliest Times to 1789*, vol. I, *History*. Tübingen: Mohr Siebeck, 1996.

Krueger, Derek, ed. *Byzantine Christianity*. People's History of Christianity 3. Minneapolis, Minn.: Fortress, 2006.

——. *Liturgical Subjects: Christian Ritual, Biblical Narrative and the Formation of Self in Byzantium*. Philadelphia: University of Pennsylvania Press, 2015.

Kruger, Stephen F. "Medieval Christian (Dis)identifications: Muslims and Jews in Guibert of Nogent." *New Literary History* 28.2 (997): 185–203.

Külzer, Andreas. *Disputationes Graecae contra Iudaeos. Untersuchungen zur byzantinischen antijüdischen Dialogliteratur und ihrem Judenbild*. Byzantinisches Archiv 18. Berlin: De Gruyter, 1999.

Laiou, Angeliki, and Roy Mottahadeh, eds., *The Crusades from the Perspective of Byzantium and the Muslim World*. Washington, DC: Dumbarton Oaks, 2001.

Langmuir, Gavin I. "Mission to the Jews and Jewish-Christian Contexts:

Scholarship and Intolerance in the Medieval Academy: Comment." *AHR* 91 (1986): 614–24.

Lauxtermann, Marc. *Byzantine Poetry from Pisides to Geometres I*. Vienna: Verlag der Österreichischen Akademie der Wissenschaften, 2003.

Lasker, Daniel J. "Jewish-Christian Polemics at the Turning-Point: Jewish Evidence from the Twelfth Century." *HThR* 89.2 (1996): 161–73.

Laurent, Vitalien, and Jean Darrouzès. *Dossier grec de l'Union de Lyon (1273–1277)*. Paris: Archives de l'Orient chrétien, 1976.

Le Coz, Raymond. *Jean Damascène. Écrits sur l'Islam*. Sources chrétiennes 383. Paris: Cerf, 1992.

Lees, Jay T. *Anselm of Havelberg: Deeds into Words in the Twelfth Century*. Leiden: Brill, 1998.

Lemerle, Paul. *Cinq études sur le XIe siècle byzantin*. Paris: Éditions du Centre National de Recherché Scientifique, 1977.

Lenski, Noel. "Power and Religion on the Frontier of Late Antiquity." In Cain and Lenski, eds. *The Power of Religion in Late Antiquity*, 1–17.

Lieu, Judith. *Constructing Early Christianity*. London: T & T Clark, 2002.

Lincoln, Bruce. *Discourse and the Construction of Society: Comparative Studies of Myth, Ritual and Classification*, 2nd ed. New York: Oxford University Press, 2014.

Lössl, Josef. "Augustine in Byzantium." *JEH* 51 (2000): 267–95.

Louth, Andrew, and Augustine Casiday, eds. *Byzantine Orthodoxies*, Society for the Promotion of Byzantine Studies Publications 12. Aldershot: Ashgate, 2006.

MacAlister, Suzanne. *Dreams and Suicides: The Greek Novel from Antiquity to the Byzantine Empire*. London: Routledge, 1996.

MacEvitt, Christopher. *The Crusades and the Christian World of the East: Rough Tolerance*. Philadelphia: University of Pennsylvania Press, 2008.

Macrides, Ruth, and Paul Magdalino. "The Fourth Kingdom and the Rhetoric of Hellenism." In *The Perception of the Past in Twelfth-Century Europe*, edited by Paul Magdalino, 117–55. London: Hambledon, 1992.

Magdalino, Paul. "Enlightenment and Repression in the Twelfth Century: The Evidence of the Canonists." In *To byzantio kata ton 12o aiona*, edited by Nicolas Oikonomides, 357–73. Athens: Hetaireia Vyzantinōn kai metavyzantinōn meleton, 1991.

——. *The Empire of Manuel I Komnenos, 1143–1180*. Cambridge: Cambridge University Press, 1993.

——. "Innovations in Government." In Mullett and Smythe, eds. *Alexios I Komnenos*, 146–66.

——. *Constantinople médiévale. Études sur l'évolution des structure urbaines*. Paris: De Boccard, 1996.

——. "Prosopography and Byzantine Identity." In *Fifty Years of Byzantine Prosopography: The Later Roman Empire, Byzantium and Beyond*, edited by Averil Cameron, 41–56. Oxford: Oxford University Press for the British Academy, 2003.

——. "Court Society and Aristocracy." In Haldon, ed., *A Social History of Byzantium*, 212–32.

——. "Cultural Change? The Context of Byzantine Poetry from Geometres to Prodromos." In Bernard and Demoen, eds., *Poetry and its Contexts*, 19–36.

——. "'All Israel will be Saved'? The Forced Baptism of Jews and Imperial Eschatology." In *Jews in Early Christian Law: Byzantium and the West, 6th to 11th Centuries*, edited by John Tolan, Nicholas de Lange, Laurence Foschia and Capucine Nemo-Pekelman, 231–42. Turnhout: Brepols, 2013.

Magdalino, Paul, and Robert Nelson. "The Emperor in Byzantine Art of the Twelfth Century." *Byzantinische Forschungen* 8 (1982): 123–83.

Mango, Cyril A. "The Conciliar Edict of 1166." *DOP* 17 (1963): 317–30.

Marciniak, Przemyslaw. "Theodore Prodromos' *Bion prasis*: A Reappraisal." *GRBS* 53 (2013): 219–39.

Markopoulos, Athanasios. "Teachers and Textbooks in Byzantium, Ninth to Eleventh Centuries." In Steckel, Gaul and Grünbart, eds. *Networks of Learning*, 3–16.

Marmodoro, Anna, and Jonathan Hill, eds. *The Author's Voice in Classical and Late Antiquity*. Oxford: Oxford University Press, 2013.

Martin, Dale B., and Patricia Cox Miller, eds. *The Cultural Turn in Late Ancient Studies: Gender, Asceticism and Historiography*. Durham, NC: Duke University Press, 2005.

Martin, John D. "Dramatical Disputations: Late Medieval German Dramatizations of Jewish-Christian Religious Disputations, Church Policy and Local Social Climates." *Medieval Encounters* 8.2 (2002): 209–27.

Mavroudi, Maria. "Learned Women of Byzantium and the Surviving Record." In *Byzantine Religious Culture: Studies in Honor of Alice-Mary Talbot*, edited by Denis Sullivan, Elizabeth Fisher and Stratis Papaioannou, 53–84. Leiden: Brill, 2012.

Messis, Charis. "Public hautement affiché et public réellement visé: le cas de l'*Apologie de l'eunuchisme* de Théophylacte d'Achrida." In Odorico, ed., *La face cachée*, 41–85.

Meyendorff, John. "Byzantine Views of Islam." *DOP* 18 (1964): 115–32.

Migliorini, Tommaso. "Teodoro Prodromo, *Amaranto*." *MEG* 7 (2007): 183–247.

——. *"Gli scritti satirici in greco letterario di Teodoro Prodromo: Introduzione, edizione, traduzione e commenti."* Ph.D diss., Scuola Normale di Pisa, 2010.

Miladinova, Nadia. *The* Panoplia Dogmatike *by Euthymios Zygadenos: A Study on the First Edition Published in Greek in 1710.* Leiden: Brill, 2014.

Miles, G. "The Representation of Reading in 'Philip the Philosopher.'" *Byzantion* 56 (2009): 292–305.

Monagle, Clare. *Orthodoxy and Controversy in Twelfth-Century Religious Discourse: Peter Lombard's* Sentences *and the Development of Theology.* Turnhout: Brepols, 2013.

Montet, Edouard. "Un ritual d'abjuration des Musulmans dans l'église grecque." *Rev. de l'histoire des religions* 53 (1906): 145–63.

Moore, Robert I. *The First European Revolution, 950–1215.* Oxford: Blackwell, 2000.

——. *The Formation of a Persecuting Society: Power and Deviance in Western Europe, 950–1250.* 2nd ed. Oxford: Blackwell, 2007.

——. *The War on Heresy: Faith and Power in Medieval Europe.* London: Profile, 2014.

Morlet, Sébastien, Olivier Munnich, and Bernard Pouderon, eds. *Les dialogues* Adversus Iudaeos. *Permanences et mutations d'une tradition polémique.* Actes du colloque international organisé les 7 et 8 décembre 2011 à l'Université de Paris-Sorbonne. Paris: Institut d'Études Augustiniennes, 2013.

Morrison, Karl F. "Anselm of Havelberg: Play and the Dilemma of Historical Progress." In *Religion, Culture and Society in the Early Middle Ages: Studies in Honor of Richard E. Sullivan,* edited by Thomas X. Noble and John J. Contreni, 219–56. Kalamazoo: Medieval Institute Publications, Western Michigan, 1987.

Muehlberger, Ellen. *Angels in Late Ancient Christianity.* Oxford: Oxford University Press, 2013.

Mullett, Margaret. "Aristocracy and Patronage in the Literary Circles of Comnenian Constantinople." In Angold, ed. *The Byzantine Aristocracy,* 173–201.

——. *Theophylact of Ochrid: Reading the Letters of a Byzantine Archbishop.* Aldershot: Variorum, 1997.

——. "Theophylact of Ohrid's *In Defence of Eunuchs.*" In Tougher, ed., *Eunuchs in Antiquity and Beyond,* 177–98.

——. "No Drama, no Poetry, no Fiction, no Readership, no Literature." In James, ed., *A Companion to Byzantine Literature,* 227–38.

——. "Whose Muses? Two Advice Poems attributed to Alexios I Komnenos." In Odorico, ed., *La face cachée,* 195–220.

Mullett, Margaret, and Dion Smythe, eds. *Alexios I Komnenos I: Papers.* Belfast: Belfast Byzantine Enterprises, 1996.

Nilsson, Ingela. "'The Same Story, but Another': A Reappraisal of Literary Imitation in Byzantium." In Schiffer and Rhoby, eds., *Imitatio – Aemulatio – Variatio,* 195–208.

——. "La douceur des dons abundants: patronage et littérarité dans la Constantinople des Comnènes." In Odorico, ed., *La face cachée,* 179–93.

——. *Raconter Byzance. La littérature au XIIe siècle.* Paris: Les Belles Lettres, 2014.

Nirenberg, David. *Anti-Judaism: The History of a Way of Thinking.* London: Head of Zeus, 2013.

Novikoff, Alex. *The Medieval Culture of Disputation: Pedagogy, Practice and Performance.* Philadelphia: University of Pennsylvania Press, 2013.

———. "Anselm of Havelberg's Controversies with the Greeks: A Moment in the Scholastic Culture of Disputation." In Cameron and Gaul, eds., *Dialogues and Debates*, forthcoming.

Obolensky, Dimitri. *The Bogomils: A Study in Balkan Neo-Manichaeism.* Cambridge: Cambridge University Press, 1948.

Odorico, Paolo. "Avant-propos." In Odorico, ed., *La face cachée*, 9.

———, ed. *La face cachée de la littérature byzantine. Le texte en tant que message immédiat.* Actes du colloque international, Paris, 5–6–7 juin 2008, organizé par Paolo Odorico en mémoire du Constantin Leventis, Dossiers byzantins 11. Paris: Centre d'études byzantines, néo-helléniques et sud-ouest européennes, École des Hautes Études en Sciences Sociales, 2012.

Odorico, Paolo, Panagiotis A. Agapitos, and Martin Hinterberger, eds. *Doux remède: poésie et poétique à Byzance.* Dossiers byzantins 9. Paris: Centre d'études byzantines, néo-helléniques et sud-ouest européennes, École des Hautes Études en Sciences Sociales, 2008.

Page, Gillian. *Being Byzantine: Greek Identity before the Ottomans.* Cambridge: Cambridge University Press, 2008.

Palau, Anna Cataldi. *"L'Arsenale Sacro* di Andronico Camatero, il proemi ed il dialogo dell'imperatore con i cardinali latini: originale, imitazioni, arrangiamenti." *REB* 51 (1993): 5–62.

Papaioannou, Stratis. *Michael Psellos: Rhetoric and Authorship in Byzantium.* Cambridge: Cambridge University Press, 2013.

———. "Voice, Signature, Mask: The Byzantine Author." In Pizzone, ed., *The Author in Middle Byzantine Literature*, 21–40.

Patlagean, Evelyne. "Aveux et désaveux d'hérétiques à Byzance (XIe–XIIe siècles)." In *L'Aveu, antiquité et moyen-âge*, 243–260. Actes de la table ronde organisée par l'Ecole française de Rome, avec le concours du CNRS et de l'Université de Trieste, Rome, 28–30 mars 1984. Rome: École française de Rome, 1986.

———. "La 'Dispute avec les Juifs' de Nicolas d'Otrante (vers 1220) et la question du Messie." In *La storia degli Ebrei nell'Italia meridionale: tra filologia e metodologia*, edited by M. G. Muzzarelli and G. Todeschini, 19–27. Bologna: Istituto per i beni artistici, culturali e naturali della Regione Emilia-Romagna, 1990.

——. "Byzance dans le millénaire médiéval." *Annales, Histoire Sciences Sociales* 60.4 (2005): 721–29.

——. *Un Moyen Âge grec. Byzance, IXe–XVe siècle.* Paris: Albin Michel, 2007.

Pizzone, Aglae, ed. *The Author in Middle Byzantine Literature: Modes, Functions and Identities.* Byzantinisches Archiv 28. Berlin: De Gruyter, 2014.

Preiser-Kapeller, Johannes. "Complex Historical Dynamics of Crisis: The Case of Byzantium." In *Krise und Transformation*, edited by Sigrid Deger-Jalkotzy and Arnold Suppan, 69–128. Beiträge des internationalen Symposiums vom 22. bis 23. November 2010 an der Österreichischen Akademie der Wissenschaften. Vienna: Verlag der Österreichischen Akademie der Wissenschaften, 2011.

Principe, Walter H. "Monastic, Episcopal and Apologetic Theology of the Papacy, 1150–1250." In Ryan, ed. *The Religious Roles of the Papacy*, 117–70.

Rapp, Claudia. "A Medieval Cosmopolis. Constantinople and its Foreign Inhabitants." In *Alexander's Revenge. Hellenistic Culture through the Centuries*, edited by Jón Ma. Asgeirsson and Nancy Van Deusen, 151–71. Reykjavik: University of Iceland Press, 2002.

Rey, André-Louis. "Remarques sur la forme et l'utilisation de passages dialogués entre chrétiens et musulmans dans le corpus de Saint Jean Damascène." In *Boukoleia. Mélanges offerts à Bertrand Bouvier*, edited by Anastasia Lazaridis, Vincent Barras, and Terpsichore Birchler, 69–83. Geneva: Editions des Belles-Lettres. 1995.

Rigo, Antonio. "Messalianismo=Bogomilismo. Un equazione dell'eresiologia medievale bizantina." *OCP* 56 (1990): 53–82.

——. "Il processo del bogomilo Basilio (1099 ca.). Una riconsiderazione." *OCP* 58 (1992): 185–211.

——. "Gli Ismaeliti e la discedenza da Abramo nella 'Refutazione del Corano' di Niceta Byzantios (meta del IX secolo)." In *I nemici della cristianità*, edited by Giuseppe Ruggieri, 83–104. Bologna: Il Mulino, 1997.

——. "Niceta Byzantios. La sua opera e il monaco Evodio." In *"In partibus Clius" Scritti in onore di Giovanni Pugliese Carratelli*, edited by Gianfranco Fiaccadori, with Andrea Gatti and Sergio Marotta, 146–87. Naples: Vivarium, 2006.

Rigo, Antonio, and Pavel Ermilov, eds. *Byzantine Theologians: The System-atization of Their Own Doctrine and Their Perception of Foreign Doctrines*. Quaderni di "Nea Rhome" 3. Roma: Università di Roma "Tor Vergata," 2009.

Robinson, Christopher. *Lucian and his Influence in Europe*. London: Duckworth, 1979.

Roilos, Panagiotis. "Amphoteroglossia: The Role of Rhetoric in the Medieval Learned Novel." In Agapitos and Reinsch, eds., *Der Roman im Byzanz*, 109–26.

——. *Amphoteroglossia: A Poetics of the Twelfth-Century Medieval Greek Novel*. Washington, DC: Center for Hellenic Studies, 2005.

Romano, Roberto. *La satira bizantina dei secoli XI–XIV: Il patriota, Caridemo, Timarione, Cristoforo di Mitilene, Michele Psello, Theodoro Prodromo, Carmi ptocoprodromici, Michele Haplucheir, Giovanni Catrara, Mazaris, La messa del glabro, Sinissario del venerabile asino*. Turin: Unione tipografico editrice torinese, 1999.

Rotman, Youval. "Christians, Jews and Muslims in Southern Italy: Medieval Conflicts in Local Perspective." In Stephenson, ed. *The Byzantine World*, 223–35.

——. "Converts in Byzantine Italy: Local Representations of Jewish-Christian Rivalry." In Bonfil, Irshai, Stroumsa, and Targam, eds. *Jews in Byzantium*, 898–922.

Rousselle, Aline. "Histoire ancienne et oubli du christianisme (note critique)." *Annales, Histoire Sciences Sociales* 47.2 (1992): 355–68.

Russell, Norman. "Anselm of Havelberg and the Union of the Churches." *Sobornorst* 1 (1979): 19–41 (first dialogue); 2.1 (1980): 29–41 (second dialogue).

Ryan, Christopher, ed., *The Religious Roles of the Papacy*: Ideals and Realities 1150–1300. Toronto: Pontifical Institute of Medieval Studies, 1989.

Safran, Linda. "A Medieval Ekphrasis from Otranto." *BZ* 83 (1990): 425–27.

——, *The Medieval Salento. Art and Identity in Southern Italy*. Philadelphia: University of Pennsylvania Press, 2014.

Salet, Gaston, ed. *Anselme de Havelberg*. Sources chrétiennes 118. Paris: Cerf, 1966.

219

Schiano, Claudio. "Il *Dialogo contro i guidei* di Nicola di Otranto tra fonti storiche e teologiche." In Morlet, Munnich and Pouderon, eds. *Les dialogues* Adversus Iudaeos, 295–317.

Scheidel, Walter, ed. *Rome and China: Comparative Perspectives on Ancient World Empires*. Oxford: Oxford University Press, 2009.

Schiffer, Elisabeth, and Andreas Rhoby, eds. *Imitatio – Aemulatio – Variatio*. Akten des internationalen wissenschaftlichen Symposiums zur byzantinischen Sprache und Literatur, Vienna 22–25 octobre 2008. Veröffentlichen zur Byzanzforschung 21. Vienna: OAW, 2010.

Schmidt, Josef. *Des Basilius aus Achrida, Erzbischofs von Thessalonich bisher unedierte Dialoge. Ein Beitrag zur Geschichte des griechischen Schismas*. Munich, 1901.

Schmitt, Jean-Claude. *La conversion d'Herman le juif: autobiographie, histoire et fiction*. Paris: Éditions du Seuil, 2003.

Schmitz, R. "Benjamin von Tudela. 'Das Buch der Reisen': Realität oder Fiktion?" *Henoch* 16 (1994): 295–314.

Schreckenberg, Heinz. *Die christlichen* Adversus Iudaeos *Texte (11.–13. Jh.)*, 4 ed. Frankfurt am Main: Peter Lang, 1999.

——. *Die christlichen* Adversus Iudaeos *Texte (11.–13.Jh.)*. 4 ed. Frankfurt am Main: Peter Lang, 1999.

Siecienski, A. Edward. *The Filioque: History of a Doctrinal Controversy*. Oxford: Oxford University Press, 2010.

Simpson, Alicia. *Niketas Choniates*. Oxford: Oxford University Press, 2013.

Simpson, Alicia and Stephanos Efthymiades, eds. *Niketas Choniates: A Historian and a Writer*. Geneva: La Pomme d'Or, 2009.

Siniossoglou, Niketas. *Radical Platonism in Byzantium: Illumination and Utopia in Gemistos Plethon*. Cambridge: Cambridge University Press, 2011.

Smythe, Dion. "Alexios I and the Heretics: The Account of Anna Komnene's *Alexiad*." In Mullett and Smythe, eds. *Alexios I Komnenos*, 232–59.

Spingou, Foteini. "Dogmatic Disputes in Constantinople: The Dialogue of Soterichos Panteugenos and its Impact." In Cameron and Gaul, eds., *Dialogues and Debates,* forthcoming.

220

Spiteris, J. "Attitudes fondamentales de la théologie byzantine, en face du role de la papauté au XIIème siècle." In Ryan, ed. *The Religious Roles of the Papacy*, 171–92.

Steckel, Sita, Niels Gaul and Michael Grünbart, eds. *Networks of Learning: Perspectives on Scholars in Byzantine East and Latin West c. 1000–1200*. Berlin and Münster: LIT Verlag, 2014.

Stephenson, Paul. "Byzantium Transformed, c. 950–1200." *Medieval Encounters* 10 (2004): 185–210.

——. "The Rise of the Middle Byzantine Aristocracy and the Decline of the Imperial State." In Stephenson, ed., *The Byzantine* World, 22–33.

——, ed., *The Byzantine World*. London: Routledge, 2010.

Stone, Andrew. "Nerses IV 'the Gracious', Manuel I Komnenos, the Patriarch Michael III Anchialos and Negotiations for Church Union between Byzantium and the Armenian Church, 1165–73." *JÖB* 55 (2005): 181–208.

——, "The Missionaries of Manuel I," *REB 66* (2008): 253–57.

Stouraitis, Ioannis. "Roman Identity in Byzantium: A Critical Approach." *BZ* 107.1 (2014): 175–220.

Stoyanov, Yuri. *The Other God: Dualist Religions from Antiquity to the Cathar Heresy*. New Haven: Yale University Press, 2000.

Stroumsa, Guy G. "Barbarians or Heretics? Jews and Arabs in the Mind of Byzantium (Fourth to Eighth Centuries)." In Bonfil, Irshai, Stroumsa, and Talgam, eds. *Jews in Byzantium*, 761–76.

Stroumsa, Sarah. *Maimonides in his World: Portrait of a Mediterranean Thinker*. Princeton: Princeton University Press, 2009.

Stroup, Sarah Culpepper. "'When I Read my Cato, it is as if Cato Speaks': The Birth and Evolution of Cicero's Dialogic Voice." In Marmadoro and Hill, eds. *The Author's Voice*, 123–51.

Teriyan, Abraham. "To Byzantium with Love: The Overtures of Saint Nerses the Gracious." In *Armenian Cilicia*, edited by Richard G. Hovannisian and Simon Payaslian, 131–57. Costa Mesa, CA: Mazda Publishers Inc., 2008

Thomas, David, et al., eds. *Christian-Muslim Relations: A Bibliographical History*. 7 vols. Leiden: Brill, 2009.

Toch, Michael. *The Economic History of European Jews: Late Antiquity and Early Middle Ages*. Leiden: Brill, 2013.

Todt, Klaus-Peter. *Bartholomaios von Edessa, Confutatio Agareni*. Corpus Islamo-Christianum, Series Graeca 2. Würzburg and Altenberge: Echter Verlag-Telos Verlag, 1988.

——. *Kaiser Johannes VI Kantakuzenos und der Islam. Politische Realität und theologische Polemik im palaiologenzeitlichen Byzanz*. Würzburger Forschungen zur Missions- und Religionswissenschaft. Religionswissenschaftliche Studien 16. Würzburg-Altenberge: Echter Verlag, 1991.

Tolan, John. "Muslims as Pagan Idolaters in Chronicles of the First Crusade." In Frassetto and Blanks, eds. *Western Views of Islam*, 97–117.

——. "Saracen Philosophers Secretly Deride Islam." *Medieval Encounters* 8.2 (2002), 184–208.

——. *Saracens: Islam in the Medieval European Imagination*. New York: Columbia University Press, 2002.

Tougher, Shaun, ed. *Eunuchs in Antiquity and Beyond* (London and Swansea, 2002).

Traninger, Anita. *Disputation, Deklamation, Dialog. Medien und Gattungen europäischer Wissensverhandlungen zwischen Scholastik und Humanismus*. Text und Kontext 33. Stuttgart: Franz Steiner Verlag, 2012.

Trapp, Erich, ed. *Dialoge mit einem "Perser."* Wiener byz. Stud. 2. Vienna: In Kommission bei G. Böhlaus, Nachf, 1966.

——. "Die Dialexis des Mönchs Euthymios mit einem Sarazenen." *JÖB* 20 (1971): 114–31

——. "Gab es eine byzantinische Koranübersetzung?" *Diptycha* 2 (1980–81): 7–17.

Trizio, Michele. "Neoplatonic Source-Material in Eustratius of Nicaea's Commentary on Book VI of the Nicomachean Ethics." In Barber and Jenkins, eds. *Medieval Greek Commentaries*, 71–109.

——. "Ancient Physics in the Mid-Byzantine Period: The *Epitome* of Theodore of Smyrna, Consul of the Philosophers under Alexius I Komnenos (1081–1118)." *Bull. de philosophie médiévale* 58 (2012): 77–99.

——. "From Anna Komnene to Dante: The Byzantine Roots of Western Debates about Aristotle's *Nicomachean Ethics*." In *Dante and the Greeks*, edited by Jan Ziolkowsky, 105–39. Washington, DC: Dumbarton Oaks, 2014.

Van Deun, Peter, and Caroline Macé, eds. *Encyclopaedic Trends in Byzantium*. Proceedings of the International Conference held at Leuven, 6–8 May 2009. Leuven: Peeters, 2011.

Van Hoof, Lieve. "Performing Greek *paideia*: Greek Culture as an Instrument for Social Promotion in the Fourth Century AD." *CQ* 63.1 (2013): 387–406.

Van Hoof, Lieve, and Peter Van Nuffelen, eds. *Literature and Society in the Fourth Century AD: Performing Paideia, Constructing the Present, Presenting the Self*. Leiden: Brill, 2014.

Wittrock, Björn. "Cultural Crystallization and World History: The Age of Ecumenical Renaissances." *Medieval Encounters* 10.3 (2004): 41–73.

Yahalom, Joseph. "The Journey Inward: Judah Halevi between Christians and Muslims in Spain, Egypt and Palestine." In de Lange, ed., *Hebrew Scholarship and the Medieval World*, 138–48.

Zacharia, Katerina, ed. *Hellenisms: Culture, Identity and Ethnicity from Antiquity to Modernity*. Aldershot: Ashgate, 2008.

Zorzi, Niccolò. "Islam e Cristianesimo durante il regno di Manuele Comneno: la disputa sul 'Dio di Maometto' nell' opera di Niketa Coniata." In *Vie per Bisanzio*, edited by Antonio Rigo, Andrea Babuin and Michele Trizio, vol. I, 275–310. VII Congresso Nazionale dell' Associazione Italiana di Studi Bizantini, Venezia, 25–28 novembre, 2009, 2 vols. Bari: Edizioni di Pagina, 2013.

Zumthor, Paul. *La lettre et la voix: De la "littérature" médiéval*. Paris: Éditions du Seuil, 1987.

Index

225

227